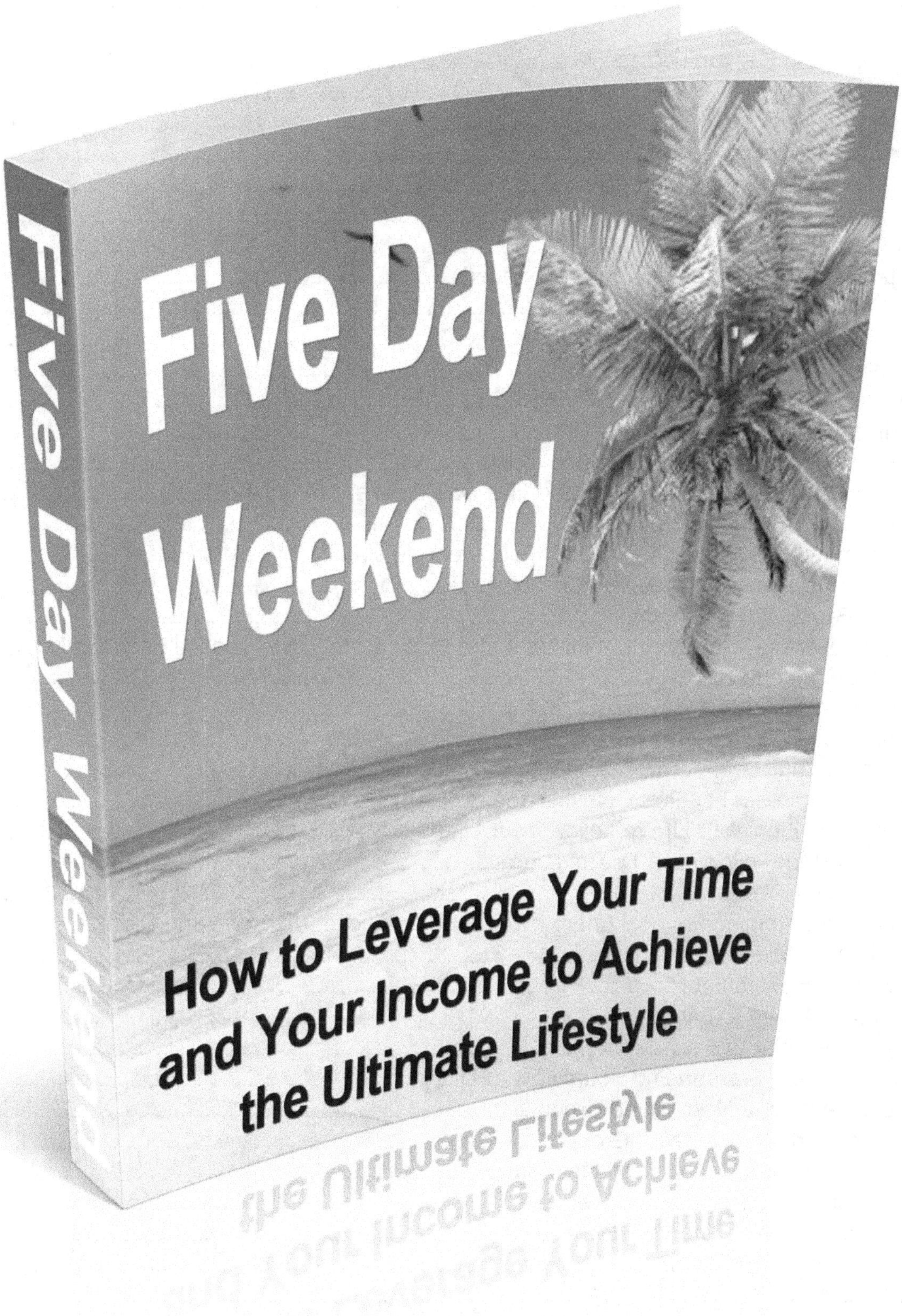
Five Day Weekend
How to Leverage Your Time and Your Income to Achieve the Ultimate Lifestyle
Five Day Weekend

Table of Contents

Introduction

Since I was 8 years old, I remember my parents packing up the family Winnebago and driving my brothers, sisters and me to a small town in Northern Michigan to vacation at my aunt and uncle's lake front cabin. Back then the five-hour drive from our home in a Detroit suburb to the cabin seemed to take forever, but the wait was always worth it.

We kids were excited about the prospect of exploring new destinations, and my parents enjoyed every minute of the open road. Over the years of my youth, we spent countless weeks roaming the back roads of America and visited every tourist trap our great country had to offer. We traveled from Michigan to Oregon, from Ohio to the Carolinas, and Florida to the Dakotas. I learned firsthand about the encompassing beauty of America and the importance of family vacations. During those early days, I fell in love with the lifestyle of spending time with family and friends and traveling.

As I grew older, I traveled to many regions of the United States both in my corporate career and in my personal life. During my 15 year career in the corporate world I began desiring a lifestyle more than just earning my paycheck. I wanted a lifestyle that would allow me to spend my time as I wanted and not by the clock on the wall. I wanted the ability to dine in world-class restaurants, travel the globe, to follow my true passions and have the income to support that lifestyle, no matter what it was.

What I discovered was that my dream lifestyle really WAS readily available. All I needed to do was decide first what type of lifestyle I wanted then create an income to support that choice. Once the choice is made the actions are simple.

Thanks to all the rapid advancements in technology and communication, enjoying Five Day Weekends is not only possible - it is a reality. Today I am a full-time lifestyle entrepreneur enjoying five day weekends every week out of the year.

A "lifestyle entrepreneur" is an individual who first designs the lifestyle they want for themselves and their family and then creates a stream of income to support that lifestyle no matter what it is. Living the lifestyle is a matter of desire, choices and decisions.

If you think enjoying Five Day Weekends and being a lifestyle entrepreneur sounds like paradise, keep reading. This book is for you.

Leverage – The Key to Success

"*Give me a lever long enough and a place to stand, and I can move the Earth.*"
– Archimedes

Leverage is a term used to explain the multiplication of an output. For example, to lift a heavy object, you have only one decision to make and that decision is to use leverage or not. You can try to lift the object directly or you can use leverage, such as a plank, crowbar or jack. Leverage is vital to success.

If I could explain the strategies and techniques used in this material with one word, that word would be leverage. Leverage is the key to the Five Day Lifestyle system. You need to leverage your time, your income and your lifestyle. You leverage your time by focusing on *what you want to do* so you can enjoy life to the fullest and *what you need to do* to provide the income to support your lifestyle. You leverage your income by adding an income multiplier. You leverage your lifestyle by combining your leveraged time and your leveraged income to achieve your desire lifestyle.

The only way to achieve your lifestyle goal is with leverage. In later chapters you learn proven strategies and techniques how to use Time Leverage, Income Leverage and Lifestyle Leverage, but for now let's take quick look at each of the three areas and learn why leverage is so vital when enjoying Five Day Weekends.

Time Leverage:

Time leverage is doing more with less. With a little fore thought and a plan you can achieve much more in a single day then most people accomplish in a week. Without time leverage you may find yourself working very hard with no noticeable advancements.

Here are the four components of time leverage you'll learn:

- Time – How to leverage your time and that of other people
- Technology – Using technology to achieve more each day
- Resources - "Little Black Book". This is your personal resource list. It's where you'll know where to look for what you need when you need it.
- Education – Using up-to-date strategies and techniques will save you time, money and frustration.

Income Leverage:

Income leverage is achieving more income with less of a time commitment that is directly attributed to the task of creating the income. For example, let's say your current hourly pay is $25 per hour. For a 40 hour work week, you'll earn $1,000 (less taxes). That is a one-to-one ratio. Another way to look at your hourly rate is you are trading one hour of your life for your current hourly pay. If you earn $25 per hour, you need to ask yourself is an hour of your life worth more? Even without knowing you personally, I would say its' worth more, much more!

Here are the four components of income leverage you'll learn:

- Creation – How to create high demand, high quality products in less time
- Technology – Using technology to increase your profit margin
- Distribution – How to get an army of people to sell your products and services
- Fulfillment – How to get your product into your customers hands without you physically touching it

Lifestyle Leverage:

Lifestyle leverage is enjoying your time and income from any location on the globe you desire. You'll be able to operate your business from your home office or from your laptop on the beach. Lifestyle leverage is the ultimate goal of the Five Day Weekend System. This is the most important area since it focuses on balancing time, income and lifestyle.

Here are the four components of lifestyle leverage you'll learn:

- Family Policy Statement – Getting family and friends important in your life to support your Five Day Weekend lifestyle
- Mindset – Finding the right balance between lifestyle and work requirements
- Physical – Maintaining physical energy with proper exercise and diet
- Masterminding – Surrounding yourself with like-minded people

What Makes This Book Different?

Implementing the strategies in the Five Day Weekend System is a proven guide to increasing your personal enjoyment of life and your cash flow. This system allows you to enjoy your life as you know you should and spend your time doing what you know you want to do.

So what makes this book different than the countless other courses and information on small business and lifestyle design available today in the marketplace? The biggest difference is that the strategies contained in this material focus on helping you to FIRST define the lifestyle you want for you and your family and then SHOW you how to create an income to support that lifestyle no matter what that lifestyle is.

Most importantly, you can use this information to design any sort of lifestyle for yourself and your family. It doesn't matter if you are a single individual wanting to travel the world or a married couple looking to leave the corporate world and work from your home office. You may be a military spouse or an individual with special lifestyle needs. It simply doesn't matter. The information in this course will first help you clearly define what you want and need from life and then will provide the income strategies and techniques to support your desires.

Everyone reading this material has a different background and different lifestyle goal. However, no matter what your lifestyle goal, you'll be able to find a directional path in this book. To fund your lifestyle you may decide become intimately involved in the day-to-day operations of your business - or you can outsource everything. It's really going to depend on what you want to achieve and accomplish and how you want to live your life.

How Do You Know This System Can Work?

With a lot of information available online from a number of different sources, it's always a good idea to learn as much as you can about a specific system and its creator. You need to know does it really work?

Here is an overview of my background and training so you'll have a better understanding of who I am.

I spent 15 years in the corporate world in the areas of real estate and financial services. In 2005 I left the corporate world and I am now a full-time lifestyle entrepreneur. While in the corporate world I earned several licenses including a real estate license, Series 7 Stockbroker license, Registered Investment Advisor designation, Life Insurance license and a Variable Annuity license. I have the corporate background and training to intelligently talk about money management and time management strategies. Since I left the corporate world in 2005, I no longer have the need to hold onto any of these licenses.

In addition, I have been a serial entrepreneur since I was 16 years old. I have owned a mail order business, a retail store, a digital publishing business and an Internet consulting business. My partners and I currently manage a number websites and we have physical products distributed on five countries around the globe and in 42 States domestically in the United States. We have several celebrity testimonials on our products. In addition, as of 2012, the products from one of our businesses have won 18 national awards over the past few years.

I drive to my office building or work from home whenever I choose. I work the hours I want and for a length of time that suits me. I don't ever have to miss my children's school activities or family events. I make my lifestyle work for me.

The reason I share this with you is not to "impress" you but to "impress upon" you that all of the information in this course has been personally tested, proven, and used to support my own Five Day Weekend Lifestyle. I have only included the collection of the best information and thrown away everything else. This information is the result of REAL WORLD experience and is not theory.

Your Lifestyle Business:

The greatest benefit of starting a lifestyle business and following the Five Day Weekend system is you'll be doing something you love. If you love your work and the lifestyle it provides, you'll soon find it's much easier, and fun, to remain motivated.

As with anything worthwhile in life, following this system does take work and persistence. It takes a plan and more importantly it takes consistent implementation of that plan. The days of starting an online business and enjoying a full time income within only a few months are over. However, with a solid plan, realistic expectations, work and some guidance you may soon find yourself enjoying the lifestyle you only dreamt of.

Unfortunately, many people may have a misconception that being a lifestyle entrepreneur and enjoying Five Day Weekends means you don't have to work. That is simply not true. It IS true that you get to DECIDE when, where and length of intervals you want to work. Would you like to run your business from your home office that is only a few steps away from your newborn's crib?

Would you like to run your business a few hours a day from your laptop computer while enjoying a two week vacation at the Beach Club Resort at Disney World? My wife and I have done that.

Would you like to run your business while traveling or while taking a leisurely road trip across the country? My wife and I have done that, too.

You see, enjoying Five Day Weekends isn't about not working; it's about balancing the requirements of work while creating a lifestyle. Remember the purpose of your lifestyle business is to provide the necessary cash flow to support your desired lifestyle.

However, owning a lifestyle business is not solely for instant gratification or personal consumption. It's more about creating a cash flow to enjoy life in the present with an eye toward the future. You see, as your business grows you are actually creating three vital components for your future. You are creating: cash flow, a lifestyle, and an asset.

Although we'll further examine each of three areas later in the book, here is a brief overview of each.

- **Cash Flow:** The positive cash flow generated from your business will support your immediate lifestyle and fund your business needs.
- **Lifestyle**: Enjoy the freedom of time to pursue your true passions.
- **Asset:** As your business grows and produces positive cash flow, you may be able to sell your business and its cash flow sometime in the future. In essence your lifestyle business itself is a vital part of your financial future.

In the corporate world the #1 goal of most employees is to retire as soon as possible so they really start to enjoy life. They are putting off the joys of the present for an unknown payoff in the future. Unfortunately, for many people who are "putting off really living" until they retire, that day may never arrive. While there are many reasons some hard working individuals may not see retirement, here are some of the more common reasons:

- Life expectancy
- Health conditions
- Not having a large enough "nest egg" to comfortably retire

By far, for many individuals the lack of necessary finances ranks top on their list. A nest egg is the amount of money an individual needs to produce the income they need to fund their retirement goals. Unfortunately, with the extreme daily volatility of the stock market since 2009 and the wide price movements of individual investments, including real estate and commodities, countless nest eggs have been completely devastated, never to return again.

A lifestyle business is a completely different scenario. You enjoy "mini-retirements" all throughout your lifetime. The term "mini-retirement" was first coin in the book *The 4-Hour Workweek: Escape 9-5, Live Anywhere, and Join the New Rich* by Tim Ferris. However, even before I learned about the term I enjoyed several "mini-retirements" so far over my life. In essence you enjoy every minute of your life in the current moment, rather than putting the big dream of retiring until some unknown date sometime in the distant future.

Traditional Retirement Planning Has Changed

While working as a registered investment advisor I helped many clients achieve the traditional financial goal of retiring. This was achieved by consistently working with clients regarding household budgeting strategies, asset allocation and quarterly reviews. In the old model of retirement planning, it worked wonders. However, since 2009 many of the old models of planning for retirement need to be re-examined. We are not saying these old strategies are bad or broken, but a new reality has set in. At the core of this new reality is the relationship between a corporation and its employees. This relationship has changed dramatically. The old model of retirement planning was based upon the belief that an individual would work for a big company for 30 or 40 years and then retire. It is much less common now for a company to maintain the same employees over 20 years, nor an employee to stay with one job for that length of time. It is a much more fluid business and employment environment.

Traditionally, employees, while working in the corporate world, would contribute to their 401k retirement plan and their employer would add money to the employee's retirement plan via a 401k matching program throughout their years of service. They would then use this money to support their lifestyle during retirement. If an individual was lucky enough, the company they worked for would also provide a pension during retirement years. As financial planners, we used these cornerstones of retirement planning to confidently make realistic projections to reach future financial goals.

However, in the current and foreseeable future, corporations will continue to eliminate pensions, reduce 401K matching options, limit annual pay raises, increase the number of layoffs and continue to aggressively outsource jobs to far-away lands. This is simply the new reality. Corporations are determined to survive. Their stockholders demand them to do so. It is the individual that must adapt to these changes.

Fortunately, with modern technology and global communication, large corporations and traditional retirement planning strategies aren't the only games in town anymore.

Let's take a quick look at six important areas and beliefs that many people still believe must be meant to enjoy a comfortable retirement.

#1: The $1 Million Dollar Nest Egg

The goal of many of my former clients was to have a $1 million portfolio the day they retired. In a rising stock market and real estate market, with annual returns of 10% or more this number was considered conservatively low. However, individuals today may need to realize that low single digit annual returns in the market may now be the norm. In addition, rising real estate values may not be as impressive in the foreseeable as in the past. Depending on the lifestyle you want to enjoy in retirement, a $1,000,000 nest egg just may not be enough.

#2: Expenses will Decrease during Retirement

Another common belief is living expenses are expected to reduce once you retire. Unfortunately, many people actually spend more their first few years of retirement. Why? They are excited, full of energy, and have more free time to focus on hobbies, travel and other interests they put off during their working years.

#3: Social Security will Help Fund Retirement

A third area many people still continue to factor into their retirement finances is social security. Currently the average social security benefit is approximately $1,200 per month. While this does help with monthly expenses, current governmental budget issues may cause future benefits to be reduced or even eliminated for future retirees.

#4: Investing in CD's and Bonds (Fixed Income Investments)

Many individuals agree that being an aggressive investor is not a good idea during retirement. Capital preservation is vital. However, being too conservative can hurt you, too. You need to consider the effects of inflation on your purchasing power and how it can be offset by your investments.

#5: The 4% Withdrawal Rate

The assumption is if you withdraw no more than 4 percent from your retirement funds you'll have enough money to last your lifetime. In a rising financial market this is a good strategy. However, over the past decade the market has been anything but rising. In addition, while inflation may be tame now, it will return and quickly eat into that 4% spending amount.

#6: Medicare Doesn't Cover Everything

Medicare is vital for those over 65 years old and for younger individuals with disabilities. While it does help with medical costs, there are also co-pays and deductibles for many treatments.

What Do We Do Now?

Now back the term "mini-retirements". Since I left the corporate world, I have became a firm believer in enjoying mini-retirements in addition to focusing on creating a "nest egg" in the future. Again the "nest egg" would be the value of the business I am building so I could either sell it sometime in the future or teach my kids how to operate it.

Basically a mini-retirement, as defined by Tim Ferris, is an extended period of ranging from four weeks to twelve weeks or longer. The goal is to have your business fund your lifestyle and give you the ability to get out of your current environment to clear your mind and get a new perspective on your life, your goals and want really matters to you. I believe the purpose of a lifestyle business to balance your work and your life so you can rejuvenate both the mind and body everyday of your life.

So let's get started...

Disillusioned with the Corporate World at Age 29

In 2005, I walked away from a six-figure income and 15 years in the corporate world to become a full-time lifestyle entrepreneur. I made a 180-degree turn and quit my job as a Registered Investment Advisor and External Mutual Fund Wholesaler to follow my true passions.

Being an external mutual fund wholesaler meant that I worked with many of the nation's leading money management firms and I was responsible for selling mutual funds and separate accounts to the financial advisor in five states in the Great Lakes region.

Even though I worked in the corporate world I worked out of my home office and I traveled over 150 nights per night and flew over 75,000 airline miles per year. I did this for almost 8 years. It was both grueling and exhilarating. This meant I only saw my family a few days week. I usually arrived back home on Friday and I would leave again on Sunday.

I began to become disillusioned with the corporate world when I was 29 years. The reason I became disillusioned wasn't due to the travel, however I did dislike being away from my family up to six days per week, but mainly with the other aspects of corporate life including the corporate politics.

You see I worked for a small, rapidly growing money management firm that was bought out by a larger firm in 1999. A few weeks after the buyout was announced a number of the employees, including several members of the external sales force, began to resign or were terminated. As it became more evident of this mass exodus, the president of the acquired company began to personally call each member of the remaining external sales force to reinsurance us that we would they had a job in the new company. He also let us know that our position wouldn't change and we could simply go on with our daily lives without the need to worry about the recent acquisition.

When the president called me, here is basically what he said:

"Hi Andy, I am calling to let you know that you have a job with the new company. You have been doing an excellent job. You have grown sales in your territory 300% over the past 12 months and you are my guy. Also, your sales manager told me that you are thinking about getting a new car and I want to reassure you that you have a job. Now go out and get the most expensive car you can afford."

After he hung up the phone, I immediately called Jen and told her about the conversation. After several minutes on the phone, Jen and decided to stop worrying about job security and within a few days I purchased a brand new, fully loaded 1999 Red Lincoln Continental.

Approximately, four weeks later, the second round of mass exodus began. In addition to several sales people leaving the company both of the National Sales Managers were no longer with the firm. From my understanding almost 40% of the external sales force had left and both national sales managers were now gone. In addition, a number of the office employees also left the organization. A few days later I received a phone call from my new National Sales Manager, a guy I never met in person and never talked with before.

Here is how the phone call basically went:

New National Sales Manager: *"Hi Andy, this is your new manager"*

Me: *"Hi"*

New National Sales Manager: *"I am calling to let you know that you no longer have a job with this company"*

Me: *"What! You have never met me in person and your firing me!"*

New National Sales Manager: *"I am calling to let you know that you no longer have a job with this company"*

Me: *"I talked with the president a month ago and he said my job was secure. He reassured me that I had a job with the new company. He even told me to go out buy the most expensive car I can afford."*

New National Sales Manager: *"I am calling to let you know that you no longer have a job with this company"*

After that brief conversation, he hung up in my ear and I was officially fired. I called the president and left a several messages over the next few days but never received a return phone call. After talking with some of the other individuals who left the company, I learned that it was rumored that one of the terms of the buyout was that a certain percentage of the external sales force had to remain on staff for a certain amount of time for the management team to receive an additional buyout bonus.

After this experience I took a six month "mini-retirement" to enjoy time with my family and really think about the future. It was during this time that Jen and I made the decision that we needed to get out of the corporate world and do our own thing. After evaluating our personal financial situation and our goals, we began looking at different opportunities and how fund our new lifestyle. During this 6 month "mini-retirement" we created an entire strategy how to move from the corporate to being lifestyle entrepreneurs and enjoying Five Day Weekends. The outline and material that I created during my "mini-retirement" I placed in this book for you to follow too.

As I mentioned I become disenchanted with corporate world at age 29, but one little thing I learned to truly value was all of the loyalty points I earned while I traveled.

Because of all of the travel I did over the years I have since qualified as a lifetime Elite member with one of the world's largest hotel chains and accumulated over 2.2 million lifetime loyalty points. I was also a member of the Gold President's circle with a rental car company and Platinum level member with one of the world's largest airlines. Being a loyalty member allows for free upgrades to bigger rooms, luxury cars, first-class seats and more. I am also a member of other programs for food, computers, clothing and more. Loyalty points makes travel and "mini-retirements" more enjoyable.

Here is a list of the loyalty points programs I have personally joined over the years. Explore each program and join the ones that make the most sense for you.

Hotels:
- Marriott - www.marriott.com - Has a global presence and offer both hotel and resort accommodations. I am a lifetime member with Marriott
- Holiday Inn – www.holidayinn.com
- Hilton Honors – www.hilton.com

Car Rental:
- Hertz – www.Hertz.com – I was President's Circle with Hertz for many years.
- National – www.NationalCar.com

Airlines:
- American Airlines www.American.com – I used to only fly Northwest Airlines until they were bought out by American. I was Platinum level with Northwest Airlines.

Food:

- Starbucks Coffee - www.Starbucks.com – Excellent place to enjoy some down time and have business meetings.
- Any local grocery store program – You have to buy food, why not join any local program near your home.

Stuff:

- BestBuy (computers, technology related) – www.bestbuy.com
- Neiman Marcus InCircle (clothing) - www.NeimanMarcus.com

2005 was the year I decided to completely leave the corporate world. I decided no matter how much money I was making it wasn't worth not spending the time in my life the way I see fit. I craved the lifestyle of traveling and seeing new places with my family and friends, watching my children grow up, but most importantly I was craving a lifestyle and not a paycheck.

I wanted to experience what life has to offer and now that I am a lifestyle entrepreneur I am now able to enjoy my time on my terms and earn the income to support my lifestyle. When you really think about it, isn't that what you want to? You want to travel, to follow your true passion and spend your time and your life as you see fit and not be the clock on the wall.

What is Lifestyle Entrepreneur?

I have used the term lifestyle entrepreneur several times and throughout the remainder of the book I'll commonly use the term, too. I would like to share with you the definition of a lifestyle entrepreneur:

"A lifestyle entrepreneur is an individual who first designs the lifestyle they want for themselves and their family, then they create a stream of income to support that lifestyle no matter what that lifestyle is."

I understand that many individuals reading this book may not look at themselves as an entrepreneur or some may even believe they may not have the skills to become a successful entrepreneur. So let's eliminate any misunderstandings of the term "lifestyle entrepreneur"

One of the best ways to completely eliminate any misunderstandings of the definition of word or term is to clearly define it. By having a precise definition, we are better able to fully understand the meaning of any word or group of words. So let's take a closer look at the definition of each of the word in the term "lifestyle entrepreneur":

Lifestyle: According to the Merriman-Webster online dictionary the term lifestyle is defined as "a particular way of living : the way a person lives or a group of people live"

No matter what you do or where you live you are currently living a certain type lifestyle. For example, if you are currently working the corporate world your lifestyle is fighting the morning commute to the office, working in an environment you may not like, dealing with corporate politics and fighting the evening commute only to arrive back home exhausted.

Many individuals living the corporate lifestyle are under constant stress and worried about job security. They are wondering if their position will be outsourced or if their entire company will relocate overseas. For many the only bright spot of the corporate lifestyle is getting two weeks of vacation so they can enjoy life the way they want to enjoy it.

Entrepreneur: According to Wikipedia, the term entrepreneur is believed to be coined by a French economist by the name of Jean-Baptiste Say in the 19th century. The broad definition of the term according the Say is "the entrepreneur shifts economic resources out of lower and into higher productivity and great yield."

In the world of the lifestyle entrepreneur "economic resources" are much more than simply money. It encompasses all aspects of life including time, money, travel, the creation of lifetime memories and the knowledge you are living life the way it should enjoyed. So let me ask you, if you are able to spend a few additional hours each day with your friends and family or pursuing your true passions instead of commuting to and from the office isn't that shifting from lower productivity tasks (sitting in traffic) to higher productivity (following your passions)? If you answered yes, you are lifestyle entrepreneur.

Now that we have defined the term Lifestyle Entrepreneur, let's take a closer look at the some of the reasons to become lifestyle business:

- Uses the business to support a lifestyle rather than primarily for the financial rewards of owning the business
- Doing meaningful work that makes a difference in their life
- Doing work that contributes back the community is some way.
- Wants flexibility of schedule and location
- Has special lifestyle needs – disabled, military spouse, etc.
- Disenchanted with the false promises of job security in the corporate world
- Unemployed, laid off or underemployed

Now compare the lifestyle business with the traditional small business model and goals:

- Solely focused on maximizing the growth and profits of the business for a future benefit. For example, the exit strategy of the management team is to sell the company once sales reach $2 million.
- Selling a product or service the management team may not completely believe in.
- Many small business owners start a business with the goal to get away from the corporate world, but they soon discovered they simply created themselves another job. They don't have the freedom of schedule or location.
- Don't fully utilize advantages in technology for outsourcing numerous tasks including product manufacturing, marketing, website design, support staff, etc.

Examining the Past to Build Your Future

Our past shapes our future
~ Author Unknown ~

Every individual reading this material has very unique life experiences. These experiences help to shape who we are today and our perspective on the future. It is these experiences that are reasons we are where we are in life. We are in our current situation and position in life because of these experiences and decisions we have made since these events occurred. Later in this chapter, I share with you an exercise to examine the events in your life and how you can use them to build a burning desire to enjoy Five Day Weekends.

The First Event that Changed My Life...

I live in a small town in Northern Michigan with a population of only about 1,500, yet despite living in this small town two separate, two intertwined events have impacted my life forever. Both of these events occurred in a city near and dear to my heart. Both of the events occurred in New York City.

September 11, 2001 will forever be remembered on a national and global scale, but also on a personal level. Like many of you reading these words, I still remember the exact location I was when I first heard the news of that fateful morning. I was in a financial advisors office in Covington, Kentucky. The quaint city of Covington is located just across the Ohio River from Cincinnati, OH. As I watched the events of the morning unfold on the television in the advisors office, the first thought that flashed through my mind was "What is happening to our country?" The second question was "Where my friends in New York City ok?"

Being in the financial services industry for a number of years I spent countless hours in New York City and over the years I made many friends. Prior to September 11, 2001 I had visited dozens of the money management firms located around Wall Street. On numerous occasions I had walked the lobbies of the World Trade Center. I traveled in corporate helicopters both departing and arriving at the Downtown Manhattan/Wall Street Heliport located at Pier 6. Pier 6 is about a 10 minute walk south of Ground Zero. Even though I was in Covington, KY over 600 miles away the events in New York City were very close. As the days passed, I learned many of the people I knew made it out safely, but I also learn that a few did not. It was soon after this event, at age 32, that further increased my desire to following my passions and living life as I saw fit.

It took over five years for me to completely transition from the corporate world to becoming a lifestyle entrepreneur. The main reason it took over five years was we were using the trial-n-error method. We spent countless hours and wasted tens of thousands of dollars figuring out what worked and didn't work. We didn't have a proven step-by-step system to follow as provided in this book. If we had the proven information contained in this book back then, I would have been able to leave the corporate world much sooner.

The Second Event and a New Mission in Life...

As I mentioned, I absolutely love New York City. Since 2001, my wife and I have traveled back to New York City on a number of occasions. We have taken the kids with us and enjoyed family vacations in Central Park. We also traveled to New York City for numerous business trips, too. So when we boarded the plane from Traverse City, Michigan to John F. Kennedy International Airport in late April, 2010 little did we know what would transpire over the next few days.

It was May 1, 2010, my wife and I were on a combination of a five day "mini-vacation" and business trip in New York City. One evening we decided to visit world famous Times Square to get some souvenirs for the kids. This was the very night of the attempted Times Square car bombing.

It was 6:30 PM EST and as we walked up Broadway toward Times Square from our hotel, little did we realize the events unfolding. A SUV, packed full of explosives, was abandoned on the side of the road near the intersection of 45th and Broadway and an anti-terrorism expert estimated the car bomb was scheduled to go off at 6:30 PM EST, the exact time my wife and I stood on that intersection.

The reason I remember the exact time is because we promised our kids we would call them at 6:30 PM EST and tell them to go to the Times Square EarthCam website so we could wave "Hi" to them from Times Square. (The Times Square EarthCam is a 24-hour live video stream of Times Square).
http://www.earthcam.com/usa/newyork/timessquare/

As Jen talked with our kids, I remember standing on the corner of 45th and Broadway looking around at the thousands of people enjoying the warm spring night in Times Square. However, what I remember the most while I stood on that corner was a five to six foot pile of black garbage bags stacked on West 45th. What I didn't notice was the SUV parked right next to the pile of trash. We were literally 30 feet away from the SUV packed full of explosives set to go off at 6:30 PM EST.

After Jen hung up the phone with the kids, we began to walk north on Broadway toward 7th and it was then we started to hear the approach of oncoming sirens. As the sirens increased in both volume and number, we realized something has happened in the immediate area.

However, we were still unaware of the potential magnitude of the event. As the sirens approached, I took a video of the first response units arriving on the scene at approximately 6:35 PM EST. We are standing on the corner of Broadway and 7th. (a block or so north of 45th and Broadway)

During the remainder of the evening I shot several on location videos including a video of Ladder #4 and supporting units. There were the first response units to arrive in Times Square at approximately 6:35 PM

Visit www.FiveDayWeekend.com/TimesSquare to watch all of the videos I personally shot the evening of May 1, 2010.

Fortunately, for us and the other people in Times Square that night, nothing happened and we didn't learn the exact details of what occurred until the next morning.

It was these two New York City experiences, in addition to being fired in 1999 that placed me on the path of enjoying Five Day Weekends. When I look back at all three of these experiences they were vital to my future. I had to experience them. These experiences helped me to clear my mind from unnecessary stress and frivolous activities and helped me to focus on what is important in life. To me the most important areas in life include:

- Following my true passions
- Spending time with family and friends
- Traveling and seeing new places
- Growing spiritually
- Challenging both my mind and my body

Getting Started: Lifestyle Business and Five Day Weekend Worksheet

Below is a worksheet to help you analysis your own life. Take time to think about your life and the main experiences and events you have lived through. They should be both positive and negative experiences. They could be the loss of job, a health issue, an extreme financial situation (positive or negative), a spiritual encounter, an exhilarating event, etc.

Look for experiences in your life that caused you to change your perspective and outlook on life. At the time the experiences occurred did they reinforce or shake your core beliefs? These are the type of experiences or events you are searching for. These are the types of experiences, when examined that can lead to great achievement and accomplishment.

Write them down and take some time to reflect about the experience. To quote the great Napoleon Hill and the author of *Think and Grow Rich*, "Every adversity, every failure, every heartache carries with it the seed on an equal or greater benefit."

After you write down these experiences ask yourself the following questions.

- How they have changed my life?
- Have these experiences put me on an unexpected or new path in life?
- Have they forced me to look at life differently?
- How did these events or experiences strengthen or shake my core beliefs?
- What did I learn from these experiences?
- Who are the people who were brought into my life as a result of these events?

Life Experience Worksheet

_____

_____

_____

_____

_____

_____

_____

_____

_____

_____

You'll use these events to provide motivation for you to follow you passion in life. Now that you have a list of events that have influenced your life and fully examined each of those experiences, the next step is to answer the following question:

"What is my true passion?" Or asked in a different way... "What type of work do I really love?"

Complete the worksheet below and really dig deep and think about what type of work do you really love to do. The answer to this question will provide direction to the type of products and service your lifestyle business will offer.

What is my true passion? – What type of work do I really love? Worksheet

_____

_____

_____

_____

_____

_____

Now you'll learn how to use these past experiences and your passion in life to empower your future. Remember, the only area of life you have complete control over is the present. You can only control the moment you are living in now. You control the current moment but the decisions you are currently making.

You can't change to past but can you learn from the past to design your future. You are where you are and who you are because of all of decisions you have made up to this exact moment in your life. Your decision making process is influenced by the events and experiences in your life. That is why the first step in designing your ideal future is to examine the events in your past, define your passion and understand how those experiences brought you to where you are today.

Now that we have examined how we got where we are today and our true passions in life, the next step is to *step off...*

Lifestyle Leverage - The Stepping Off Point

Faith is taking the first step even when you don't see the whole staircase.
~ Martin Luther King, Jr. ~

At the beginning of this material I explained three components of leverage. These were Time leverage, Income leverage and Lifestyle leverage. The purpose of the Five Day Weekend system is to teach you how to first design a lifestyle and then create an income to support that lifestyle. Thus, the stepping off point in realizing your goal is Lifestyle leverage. This is the first area we will focus on.

The four components of the Lifestyle Leverage are:

- Family Policy Statement – Getting family and friends important in your life to support your Five Day Weekend lifestyle
- Mindset – Finding the right balance between lifestyle and work requirements
- Physical – Maintaining physical energy with proper exercise and diet
- Masterminding – Surrounding yourself with like-minded people

Create a Family Policy Statement

The happiest moments of my life have been the few which I have passed at home in the bosom of my family.
~ Thomas Jefferson ~

The first step to living your Five Day Weekend is to create a Family Policy Statement (FPS). Creating a family policy statement is much like creating an Investment Policy Statement (ISP). An investment policy statement is a document that describes how you will invest your money. It provides guidance and direction to the type of investments you invest in, but more importantly it provides a framework with what you won't invest your money in. It gives you a clear and comprehensive plan to base your decisions. It also prevents you from making random and panicky decisions based upon short-market volatility. Best of all it helps to remove the emotion from the equation.

A family policy statement forces you to put your strategies in writing and commit to a disciplined approach to achieving your lifestyle goals.

Creating a FPS is probably the most important decision you can make since it keeps you disciplined. In addition, it helps you to remain focused in your areas expertise and prevents you from chasing the "next shiny object". I know, it may sound like a long and drawn out experience, but it doesn't have to be that way. A FPS is simply a few pages that you complete on an annual basis and every year after. You simply review and update it on an annual basis to reflect your current lifestyle and goals.

Like with an investment statement, the family policy or mission statement would include your objectives, your time horizon and even your risk tolerance. Read through the example below just to get an idea of the type of information to include in your FPS. However, don't worry about fully completing this until you have finished reading the entire book. The reason is at this point you simply won't have the answers to the questions in the FPS until you finish this material and when you do have the answers, this is the format to follow.

I'll fully explain how to research all of the areas in the FPS in each of the following chapters.

Take calculated risks. That is quite different from being rash.

~ George Patton ~

The process of creating a family policy statement helps you understand the "how" to get started in enjoying Five Day Weekends. It also builds helps you to build a support network and a group of people who will be able to help you in almost any aspect of your lifestyle. Any individual that your decision affects should be involved with the creation of the family policy statement. You don't need to disclose intimate details about your business, but general only information so they understand why you are doing what you're doing so they can help.

For example, you're a single 20-something individual, your decision to become a lifestyle entrepreneur will still affect some people in your immediate life. What happens if you are running your business during a four week trip in the Yucatan and drink the ground water? The water table in the Yucatan is very close to the surface and may be contaminated by garbage runoff. If you get sick who will you call if you are in the hospital? Will it be a sibling, your grandmother, your dad, or a close friend? These people need to be supportive of your new lifestyle, since you won't want them to be giving you a lecture if you are sick in a hospital bed halfway across the globe. You don't need the stress.

Or...

You have a husband and two children in your life or maybe you and your spouse are retired. You and your family should be in complete agreement with your lifestyle. Some people even involve extended family members or friends in the process. Their support may remove any potential stress and their knowledge and contacts may be invaluable as you launch your new lifestyle.

Once you complete the family policy statement, everyone should sign it. You're then ready to launch your adventure with the whole crew on board. You and the important people in your life must be in complete agreement. You need to involve your spouse, your children, etc., in your decision-making process. This will ensure everyone affected by your decision will know when, where, and why you are doing what you're doing.

A example and a blank Family Policy Statement is provided on the following pages for your use.

Example of a Family Policy Statement (Don't worry about some of the terms or strategies used in this example, I'll fully explain them and show you how to implement them in later chapters)

Purpose of Five Day Weekend Lifestyle
The purpose of my Five Day Weekend lifestyle business is to provide an immediate and growing cash flow that will allow me to travel the globe two weeks a month and also work from my home office.

Lifestyle Expectations
We expect to travel and work from our desired destinations, remodel a room in our house annually and buy a new car every five years.

Cashflow Expectations
We expect our annual cash flow to be $75,000 from affiliate websites and $25,000 from selling our products at street fairs.

Time Horizon
Our target date to become a full time lifestyle entrepreneur is two years. We expect to have 12 affiliate websites created (three per quarter). We expect to have attended 8 street fairs (two per quarter)

Niche Allocation

We will have websites in the following niches: Financial Services (credit card applications, insurance quotes, etc.) 33%, Health and Wellness – 33%, Technology (Mobile Phone services, Internet Services, Social Media courses, etc.) – 33%. We will sell the following products at streets fair: clothes, purses and outdoor signs (man cave signs, etc.)

Rebalancing

Due to my background and professional training, the website portfolio with maintain the above allocation. Prior to adding a new website to any niche, we'll look to add to website to other another niche to manage our income and niche exposure risk.

Income Sources

We will focus on both digital downloadable products and physical products to sell.

- **Digital Download Products:** Affiliate programs, CPA programs and Adsense.
- **Physical Products:** Private label products. We will source all of our products from the website Alibaba.com

Sales Channels

We will focus on selling products (physical and digital) in the following channels:
- Ebay (Physical products)
- Clickbank (Digital products)
- Street Fairs (Physical products)
- Amazon Kindle (Digital products)
- Google Adwords (Digital and Physical products)
- Facebook Ads (Digital and Physical products)
- Street Fairs (Physical products)

Our business will avoid: spammy email marketing, website flipping strategies and banner advertising.

Education

We will subscribe to the following magazines: Internet Retailer, Website Magazines, Enterpreneur. We will view the following websites: www.FiveDayWeekend.com

Signature: _____ Date: /   /

Signature: _____ Date: /   /

Signature: _____ Date: /   /

Note: This simplified FPS is for illustration purposes only. Use the blank form below to customize your goals and needs. The actual dollar amounts and specific dates are for illustration only.

Purpose of Five Day Weekend Lifestyle

_____

_____

_____

_____

Lifestyle Expectations

_____

_____

_____

_____

Cashflow Expectations

_____

_____

_____

_____

Time Horizon

_____

_____

_____

_____

Niche Allocation

_____

_____

_____

_____

Rebalancing

_____

_____

_____

_____

Income Sources

_____

_____

_____

_____

Sales Channels

We will focus on selling products (physical and digital) in the following channels:

- _____
- _____
- _____
- _____
- _____
- _____
- _____

Our business will avoid:

_____

_____

_____

_____

Education

_____

_____

_____

_____

Signature: _____ Date: / /

Signature: _____ Date: / /

Signature: _____ Date: / /

Lifestyle Leverage – Creating the Mindset and Finding the Right Balance Between Lifestyle and Work Requirements

Those who do certain things in this Certain Way, whether on purpose or accidentally, get rich; while those who do not do things in this Certain Way, no matter how hard they work or how able they are, remain poor
~ Wallace D. Wattles ~

The Five Day Weekend system is all about "doing certain things in a certain way". When you adjust your mindset to only attract certain thoughts and only pursue certain activities, your lifestyle will soon follow. By keeping your mind focused on what you want your lifestyle to be, you will find yourself eagerly and swiftly doing only those things that bring you closer to your ultimate goal. Everything starts with the proper mindset.

However, unless you're independently wealthy, the Five Day Weekend lifestyle you are envisioning may seem out of reach, just a dream that you'd love to see come true. To that I ask, "How badly do you want it?" Only you can answer that question, but time and time again, history has shown that people who know what they want and focus their mind on these goals have achieved success more often than not.

Mountains are climbed. Rivers are conquered. Records are set. The man or woman of your dreams says, "I do." These achievements occur because one of the benefits of being human is our ability to choose among the many opportunities that present themselves each day and because somebody made a choice. Your Five Day Weekend lifestyle is much the same. You can choose to pursue your Five Day Weekend lifestyle or not. However, in the final moment of your life your choices will be no more. At the end of your life would you rather say, "I'm glad I did" or "I wish I would have?" It's all about mindset. When you have the mindset of "I'm glad I did", you'll always be on the lookout for those activities, people and experiences that will bring your closer to your desire lifestyle. You'll be proactive, rather than reactive. You'll be searching for great accomplishments? Great accomplishments can be any achievement including but not limited to playing with your kids, a daily walk on the beach with your spouse, filing for a patent or trademark or closing the deal for a new $100,000 client.

So how are great accomplishments achieved? In the moment of decision, you weigh the potential benefits of various courses of action against the potential costs.

Sometimes the choices are between a course of action that offers the least amount of risk or the greatest amount of reward. Great accomplishments occur when the latter path is chosen. While not every decision we are faced with everyday is one that carries the weight of tremendous achievement, we all still strive to make decisions that will be the most beneficial to us and to those we love. So, with all the decisions you encounter every day, is there a secret to making the right one every time? Yes, there is.

The secret to making the right decision every time is to determine what will take you closer to your lifetime goal. Did you notice I wrote "lifetime goal" and not "long-term goal?" The difference between the two is vast. Long-term goals are things you would like to accomplish. Lifetime goals are things you must accomplish. These are goals that you want to achieve no matter what it takes.

One of the best ways to determine the difference between your lifetime goals and your long-terms goal is ask yourself the following question: "If I knew I was going to die one year from today, what would I want to accomplish?" One year is a very good length of time because it gives you the time you need to achieve your goals, yet it limits how much time you can waste.

So, "What are your lifetime goals?"

Lifetime Goals

If you already have a list of lifetime goals waiting on the tip of your tongue, it's time to put them in ink. Writing down your goals is a time-tested tactic for the achievement of success that has been replicated by everyone from self-help guru Anthony Robbins to actor Jim Carrey. It worked for them. It can work for you.

If you don't already have a list of lifetime goals that you can rattle off at the drop of a hat, it's time to get one. Take your time and really think about the things that are important to you. Write down everything you want to accomplish in your life ranging from your ideal weight, the places you want to travel, your monthly income, etc. Don't hold anything back. This is your wish list of life. It's your grab bag of everything you want from life.

Here are few examples from my list of lifetime goals:

- "Mini-Retirement" in Hawaii
- Walk on the Great Wall of China
- Visit all 50 States (I have been to 42 States)
- Meet my great grand children
- Finish a marathon
- Meet the President of United States (doesn't matter political affiliation of the President. I just think it would be cool to meet the President of the United States) *BTW: I have personally attended two presidential speeches.*
- Create a really cool invention
- Learn how to paint
- Learn how to surf
- Swim with the dolphins
- Share a glass of wine with my wife at our 75th wedding anniversary
- Eat only fresh fruits and vegetables for 7 days
- Volunteer to help build a Habitat for Humanity House
- Ride a rocket into space
- Learn to speak Spanish and Arabic

Take all of the time you need to create your list. Once you've got your list, write it down and don't look at it for 24 hours. When you see the list again, decide if there's anything on it that you want to change. Repeat the process as many times as possible until the goals on your list represent your lifetime goals. This exercise will begin to form your lifestyle mindset.

Use the blank lines that follow to write your lifetime goals. Remember, believe anything is possible.

_____

_____

_____

_____

_____

_____

_____

_____

_____

_____

Prioritize Your Lifetime Goals

Now that you have a list of your lifetime goals, it's time to put your goals in order. Prioritizing your goals will help you determine if there are areas of your life that must be addressed first in order to make it possible to achieve your other goals. Write your prioritized list below:

1. _____
2. _____
3. _____
4. _____
5. _____
6. _____
7. _____
8. _____
9. _____
10. _____

Once you have you have prioritized your goals the next step is to categorize your goals into five main areas of life. The five main areas for most people include:

1. Social – Friends, relatives, family members, etc.
2. Health – Food, exercise, etc.
3. Spiritual – Mental growth, personal growth, etc.
4. Community – Giving back time or resources, etc.
5. Financial – Cash flow, work environment, etc.

The reason you want to categorize your goals into each of the five areas is the create goal synergy. Goal synergy is the energy that is created so the final output of two or more elements is greater than the sum of the individual parts.

For example, let's say your goal for starting a lifestyle business is to work from home so you can spend time with you three-year old son. In addition, you also want to donate both time and money to a local charity organization.

Your lifestyle business will create the following synergy:

- Your "social" aspect, spending more time with your son, combined with the "community" aspect, the ability to donate time, as well as the "financial" aspect, the ability to donate money to an organization you believe in, is an example of goal synergy. You see, as a lifestyle entrepreneur, your business gives you the ability to create synergy in every aspect of your life.

Now let's look at the same scenario but instead of being a lifestyle entrepreneur you work in the corporate world.

- Your "social" goal to spend more time is limited with how much time you need to spend away from your home and family. You need to be in the office from 9 to 5 everyday, while a day care provider is taking care of your son.
- The "community" goal to donate time also is dependent upon the corporate world. You simply can't leave work at 2:00 PM on Thursday afternoon to volunteer at your favorite charity. If you do, you may get fired from your job.
- The "financial" aspect may or may not be affected by your corporate job. You may have the money to donate to the organization, but will donating money give you the complete fulfillment you are seeking?

Social Goals:

1. _____

2. _____

3. _____

4. _____

5. _____

6. _____

7. _____

8. _____

9. _____

10. _____

11. _____

12. _____

13. _____

14. _____

15. _____

16. _____

17. _____

18. _____

19. _____

20. _____

Health

1. _____

2. _____

3. _____

4. _____

5. _____

6. _____

7. _____

8. _____

9. _____

10. _____

11. _____

12. _____

13. _____

14. _____

15. _____

16. _____

17. _____

18. _____

19. _____

20. _____

Spiritual

1. _____

2. _____

3. _____

4. _____

5. _____

6. _____

7. _____

8. _____

9. _____

10. _____

11. _____

12. _____

13. _____

14. _____

15. _____

16. _____

17. _____

18. _____

19. _____

20. _____

Community

1. _____

2. _____

3. _____

4. _____

5. _____

6. _____

7. _____

8. _____

9. _____

10. _____

11. _____

12. _____

13. _____

14. _____

15. _____

16. _____

17. _____

18. _____

19. _____

20. _____

Financial

1. _____

2. _____

3. _____

4. _____

5. _____

6. _____

7. _____

8. _____

9. _____

10. _____

11. _____

12. _____

13. _____

14. _____

15. _____

16. _____

17. _____

18. _____

19. _____

20. _____

Now that you have identified your true inner desires, how do you reposition your life and build the mindset so you can enjoy Five Day Weekends? The first step in repositioning your life is to conquer the biggest obstacle you'll face as you decide to pursue your lifetime goal. For many, the biggest challenge you will face when making changes to your life is dealing with the opinions and criticisms of others.

Live Life on Your Own Terms

"Who does he think he is to start his own business?" you'll likely hear others say. "He has a wife and family to support. Why doesn't he just get a real job like everybody else?" or "She's 50 years old, she can't just travel all over the world and operate her business from hotel rooms. She can't just run off and do anything she wants to do."

Other people's opinions and criticisms arise anytime you do something that is outside the critic's comfort zone. If you're a skydiver, somebody will say, "That's dangerous." If you set out to write a book, somebody will say, "That's a waste of time." Other people's opinions and criticisms are like heavy chains that drag you down and hold you back from achieving your goals. If you listen to the critics, they will rob you of your happiness and stop you from reaching your goals.

A Story about Other People's Opinions and Criticisms

I once knew a widow named Henrietta who owned 20 acres of development real estate in addition to her primary residence. Her deceased husband's sister owned the neighboring 20-acre parcel. When they first purchased the property, the goal was to build a shopping center and a number of other outbuildings on the property. Henrietta and her husband were going to use the cash flow generated from this real estate development to fund their retirement years. However, after they purchased the property, Henrietta's husband passed away and she wasn't much interested in developing the shopping center without her husband. So the years passed and the 20 acres remained vacant.

Henrietta had always wanted a spiral staircase to the second story of her home. However, she and her husband never got around to building it. At the time we met Henrietta was thinking about selling her 20 acres and using the money to build her dream staircase and travel the world.

When her children and her sister-in-law learned what she was considering, they made her life miserable. The children called her up almost every day and told her that they were entitled to the vacant property. Her sister-in-law called on the days her kids didn't and told her that she thought her brother would want the property to stay in the family.

The sister-in-law also told Henrietta that if she did sell it, it wouldn't be right for her to make a profit. The sister-in-law demanded it be sold to her at the original purchase price. The market price per acre was approximately $15,000, and the original cost was about $500 per acre.

Henrietta let these other people's opinions eat her up inside. The kids weren't interested in their mother's dreams of building a staircase and traveling; they were only waiting for their inheritance. The sister-in-law wanted the property so she could own the whole 40 acres. The market value of the entire 40-acre parcel would be worth over $500,000.

Since I lost touch with Henrietta, I never did learn whether she built her dream staircase or gave in to the pressure. The worst part of this story is that the complaints from Henrietta's critics originated from their own greed, discomfort, and insecurity. Remember when people criticize you, their comments usually stem from an unresolved issue within themselves. So don't worry what other people think, do, or say. Remember, it's your life, not theirs.

How to Reposition Your Life to Follow Your Lifetime Goals

Now that you have rediscovered your life passions by using the worksheets, how do you reposition your life to follow your goals? The answer is simple, yet many won't do it. The answer: Do whatever it takes. If you absolutely know what your destiny is, the only person you can fail is yourself. Go for it!

Getting Started: Follow Your Dreams

After my wife Jennifer and I graduated from college, we moved to a small town in Northern Michigan. In our life together, Jen and I both agree that the most important component of our lifestyle is living in a small town in Northern Michigan. Although, we both enjoy traveling and meeting new people our core foundation is enjoying the serenity of a small town. So we built our lifestyle around living in a small town and molding life around this deep-seated desired.

At that time we move to small town in Northern Michigan, neither of us had a job. Jennifer was 22 years old, and I was 23. We had $500 in the bank and $5,000 in credit card debt. We moved on December 31, 1992. It was the worst day of the year to travel. The I-75 Expressway (one of the North and Southbound expressways in Michigan) was covered with icy snow, and a howling blizzard poured sleet and freezing rain on us during the entire trip. At one point, the wind was so strong it pushed my pick-up truck off the road and into a snow bank. Fortunately, my truck and cargo were undamaged. But our psyches were. We weren't even settled in yet and had started to reconsider our decision to move to a small Northern town. Would the winters always be this cruel? Would we need to buy a four-wheel drive truck? Had we made the wrong decision? These and many other questions raced through our minds as we inched our way north on I-75. Twenty years later, we wouldn't change our location for any reason. We love where we live, and the lifestyle we have.

When we moved, we didn't have jobs, we didn't have money, and we didn't have a plan; however, we did have a goal. The goal was simple. We wanted to build our future in the pristine beauty of Northern Michigan. Once we moved, our plan emerged—to put food on the table and a roof over our heads.

The first few years were the toughest because we were a young couple with credit card debt, car payments, and rent to pay. We worked many different jobs to make ends meet. At first, that was any job that paid the bills. My initial job was selling timeshare real estate at a local resort. Jennifer worked through a temporary employment agency as a secretary. Since our bills were high and our income was low, we both moonlighted to keep food on the table. In addition to my day job, I mowed lawns, plowed driveways and shoveled snow off roofs. Jennifer worked nights as a bookkeeper. With all that, we had a combined income of approximately $28,000 during our first year.

A few years later, I chose to enhance my career. To reach this goal, I worked in another state Monday through Friday. I saw my wife and young family only on weekends. I drove six hours home each Friday, and another six hours back to work each Sunday. This difficult situation lasted for an entire year until I was to operate my territory out of my home office. But our commitment to enjoy our lifestyle was so fierce, we wouldn't even consider changing even as our friends increasingly questioned our sanity. Many didn't understand why we would willingly "starve" to enjoy the freedom of lifestyle.

As time passed, we created more concrete personal and financial goals for ourselves. When we created goals and our lives became more focused, our income and enjoy of life increased. Twenty years after our move, we are better off financially than many of our friends. In addition, we are stronger as a couple because we weathered, together, those tougher financial and emotional times. It's been a long, hard road to travel. However, we wouldn't trade our experience for a million dollars. We have survived the toughest of times and know the future can't be any harder than the past. We have no regrets.

To us, living the Five Day Weekend lifestyle is worth the sacrifice of not having a "real" job. I did the corporate grind for 15 years. I experienced firsthand brutal corporate politics and being fired from a six-figure job.

Being lifestyle entrepreneurs, we are able to connect to something bigger than ourselves. We have a deep realization that we're enjoying all that life has to offer. All of this is due to the ability to enjoy Five Day Weekends. We are able to enjoy "mini-retirements". We can shut off the computers and mobile phones to take a leisurely stroll along the beach in the middle of the day if life gets to stressful.

Do Whatever it Takes

When it comes to achieving your goals, knowing what you should do is usually the easiest step; the remaining steps are the hard ones. However, once you know what you need to do, the next step is to get out into the world and do it. The only question remaining is: Do you have the courage?

Courage is taking an action you know you must do in order to accomplish a goal. It's about repeatedly stepping outside of your comfort zone until you can take that step with confidence. Countless examples of courage can be found everyday in our Armed Forces. These men and women know they must perform tasks that are sometimes outside of their comfort zones. I'm sure the first time an Army Special Forces Ranger parachutes from an airplane, there is a brief moment of being outside his comfort zone, but he keeps doing it until he is ranked among the elite of our fighting forces.

You and I can tap into this outstanding quality we call courage. Of course, the line between courage and foolishness is a thin one. Take it from someone who knows. For this reason, I strongly suggest that you do not quit your job and venture out to pursue your Five Day Weekend lifestyle in the middle of a blizzard.

Courage is much easier to demonstrate when you have the physical energy to embark upon your goals. While this book is not about book about physical diet and exercise but you still the have the mindset for a healthy lifestyle. In the next section, we'll learn more about creating the mindset to provide the energy you need.

Physical – Maintaining Physical Energy with Proper Mindset, Exercise and Diet

Physical – The Proper Mindset

In order to enjoy a healthy body and healthy mind you must have a mindset that you are naturally healthy. No matter what your past health issues have been or what your current health issues are now, you are naturally healthy. All of us have different degrees of being health. Being healthy is a very individualized experience. For some people, having a body mass index (BMI) of 15 is extremely healthy, other people more be or more less.

The goal of being health is not to try to look like a runway model, but to have your body reflect your concept of being healthy. Of course, certain guidelines are always a good idea to keep in mind. For example, eat anti-oxidant rich foods, get a well balanced diet, follow an individualized exercise routine and get enough sleep. Thus the first step in being healthy is to enter into complete thought connection with health.

The best way to do this is to form a mental image or picture of yourself as being well, imagining a perfectly strong and healthy body; and to spend sufficient time in contemplating this image to make it your habitual thought of yourself.

This is not so easy as it sounds; it necessitates the taking of considerable time for meditation, and not all persons have the imaging faculty well enough developed to form a distinct mental picture of themselves in a perfect or idealized body. Form a mental image of how you want to your body to look at the age you are now.

It is not necessary or essential, however, to have a clear mental image of yourself as you wish to be; it is only essential to form a conception health, and to relate yourself to it. This conception of health is not a mental picture of a particular thing; it is an understanding of health, and carries with it the idea of perfect functioning in every part and organ.

You may picture yourself as perfect in body shape, that helps, but more importantly you must think of yourself as doing everything in the manner of a perfectly strong and healthy person. You can picture yourself as walking down the street with an erect body and a vigorous stride; you can picture yourself as doing your day's work easily and with surplus vigor, never tired or weak; you can picture in your mind how all things would be done by a person full of health and power, and you can make yourself the central figure in the picture, doing things in just that way.

Never think of the ways in which weak or sickly people do things, always think of the way strong people do things. Spend your leisure time in thinking about the strong way, until you have a good conception of it and always think of yourself in connection with the strong way of doing things. That is what I mean by having a maintain physical energy.

In order to establish perfect functioning in every part of your body, man does not have to study anatomy or physiology, so that he can form a mental image of each separate organ and address himself to it. He does not have to "treat" his liver, his kidneys, his stomach, or his heart. There is one component of health in man, which has control over all the involuntary functions of his life and the thought of perfect health, impressed this upon your mind and it will reach each part and organ.

The transformation of the physical body into the image of the ideal held by the mind-body is not accomplished instantaneously. We cannot transfigure our physical bodies at will. It takes time to see noticeable changes so be patient. Holding only thoughts of perfect health will ultimately cause perfect functioning; and perfect functioning will in due time produce a perfectly healthy body.

Physical – How to Eat

As simple as it is, it is a fact that man naturally chews his food. And if it is natural that we should chew our food, the more thoroughly we chew it the more completely natural the process must be. If you will chew every mouthful to a liquid, you need not be in the least concerned as to what you shall eat, for you can get sufficient nourishment out of any ordinary food.

Whether or not this chewing shall be an irksome and laborious task or a most enjoyable process, depends upon the mindset and mental attitude in which you come to the table.

If your mind and attitude are on other things, or if you are anxious or worried about business or other areas of life you will find it almost impossible to eat without swallowing without chewing your food. You must learn to live that while you are eating you will have no worries while you are eating. It's an excellent habit to give your undivided attention to the act of eating while at the table.

When you eat, do so with an eye single to the purpose of getting all the enjoyment you can from that meal. Forget any worries from your mind and focus all of your attention on the meal. This will not only allow you to enjoy your food, but you'll also find that you'll have none of "pit in the stomach" feeling after you complete your meal.

Do not select some food because you think it will be good for you; select that which will taste good to you. If you are to get well and stay well, you must drop the idea of doing things because they are good for your health, and do things because you want to do them. Select the food you want most. The get enjoyment out of how to eat, you should also take all types of food, healthy or tasty, in moderation.

Do not fix your attention on the act of chewing; fix it on the TASTE of the food; and taste and enjoy it until it is reduced to a liquid state and passes down your throat by involuntary swallowing. No matter how long it takes, do not think of the time. Think of the taste. Do not allow your eyes to wander over the table, speculating as to what you shall eat next. Do not worry for fear there is not enough, and that you will not get your share of everything. Do not anticipate the taste of the next thing. Instead focus your mind centered on the taste of what you have in your mouth. And that is all of it.

Scientific and healthful eating is a delightful process after you have learned how to do it, and after you have overcome the bad old habit of gobbling down your food unchewed. It is best not to have too much conversation going on while eating; be cheerful, but not talkative; do the talking afterward.

When you sit down to the table enjoy your food and the people you are eating it with. When I worked in the corporate world, I commonly conducted lunch meetings and dinner meeting daily with clients and potential clients. During these meals, I made it a point not to bring up the subject of business until 75 percent of the food was eaten. This meant for the first 30 – 45 minutes of the meeting we talked about everything except business. We talked about family, places we wanted to visits, the restaurant and more. This practice made eating more enjoyable.

In most cases, some use of your willpower is required to form the habit of correct eating. The habit of swallowing unchewed food is an unnatural one, and is without doubt mostly the result of fear. Fear that we will be robbed of our food. We fear that we will not get our share of the good things We fear that we will lose precious time. These are the causes of haste. Then there is anticipation of dessert, and the consequent desire to get at them as quickly as possible.

Never eat until you have an earned hunger, no matter how long you go without food. This is based on the fact that whenever food is needed in the system, if there is power to digest it, the sub-conscious mind announces the need by the sensation of hunger. Learn to distinguish between genuine hunger and the gnawing and craving sensations caused by unnatural appetite.

Hunger is never a disagreeable feeling, accompanied by weakness, faintness, or gnawing feelings at the stomach; it is a pleasant, anticipatory desire for food, and is felt mostly in the mouth and throat. It does not come at certain hours, it only comes when the sub-conscious mind is ready to receive, digest, and assimilate food.

Eat whatever foods you want, within moderation, making your selection from as much fresh food as possible. Each of us is guided to the type foods that is right for each of us. I am referring, of course, to the foods which are taken to satisfy hunger, not to those which have been contrived merely to gratify appetite or a "sweet tooth". If eating is successfully done, digestion and the building of a healthy body are successfully begun.

Physical – When to Eat

You cannot build and maintain a perfectly healthy body by mental action alone, or by the performance of the unconscious or involuntary functions alone. There are certain actions, more or less voluntary, which have a direct and immediate relation with the continuance of life itself; these are eating, drinking, breathing, and sleeping. No matter what man's thought or mental attitude may be, he cannot live unless he eats, drinks, breathes, and sleeps; and, moreover, he cannot be well if he eats, drinks, breathes, and sleeps in an unnatural or wrong manner. It is therefore vitally important that you should learn the right way to perform these voluntary functions, and I shall show you this way, beginning with the matter of eating, which is most important.

There has been a vast amount of controversy as to when to eat, what to eat, how to eat, and how much to eat; and all this controversy is unnecessary, for the Right Way is very easy to find. You have only to consider the Law which governs all attainment, whether of health, wealth, power, or happiness; and that law is *that you must do what you can do now, where you are now; do every separate act in the most perfect manner possible, and put the power of faith that you will achieve your goal into every action*.

The processes of digestion are under the supervision and control of an inner division of man's mentality, which is generally called the sub-conscious mind; and I shall use that term here in order to be understood. The sub-conscious mind is in charge of all the functions and processes of life; and when more food is needed by the body, it makes the fact known by causing a sensation called hunger. Whenever food is needed, and can be used, there is hunger; and whenever there is hunger it is time to eat. When there is no hunger it is unnatural and wrong to eat, no matter how great may APPEAR to be the need for food. Even if you are in a condition of apparent starvation, with great emaciation, if there is no hunger you may know that FOOD CANNOT BE USED, and it will be unnatural and wrong for you to eat. Though you have not eaten for days, weeks, or months, if you have no hunger you may be perfectly sure that food cannot be used, and will probably not be used if taken. Whenever food is needed, if there is power to digest and assimilate it, so that it can be normally used, the sub-conscious mind will announce the fact by a decided hunger. Food, taken when there is no hunger, will sometimes be digested and assimilated, because Nature makes a special effort to perform the task which is thrust upon her against her will; but if food be habitually taken when there is no hunger, the digestive power is at last destroyed, and numberless evils caused.

If the foregoing be true—and it is indisputably so—it is a self-evident proposition that the natural time, and the healthy time, to eat is when one is hungry; and that it is never a natural or a healthy action to eat when one is not hungry. You see, then, that it is an easy matter to scientifically settle the question when to eat. ALWAYS eat when you are hungry; and NEVER eat when you are not hungry.

We must not fail, however, to make clear the distinction between hunger and appetite. Hunger is the call of the sub-conscious mind for more material to be used in repairing and renewing the body, and in keeping up the internal heat; and hunger is never felt unless there is need for more material, and unless there is power to digest it when taken into the stomach. Appetite is a desire for the gratification of sensation. A normally fed person cannot have a hunger for candy or sweets; the desire for these things is an appetite. You cannot hunger for tea, coffee, spiced foods, or for the various taste-tempting devices of the skilled cook; if you desire these things, it is with appetite, not with hunger. Hunger is nature's call for material to be used in building new cells, and nature never calls for anything which may not be legitimately used for this purpose.

Appetite is often largely a matter of habit; if one eats or drinks at a certain hour, and especially if one takes sweetened or spiced and stimulating foods, the desire comes regularly at the same hour; but this habitual desire for food should never be mistaken for hunger. Hunger does not appear at specified times. It only comes when work or exercise has destroyed sufficient tissue to make the taking in of new raw material a necessity.

For instance, if a person has been sufficiently fed on the preceding day, it is impossible that he should feel a genuine hunger on arising from refreshing sleep. In sleep the body is recharged with vital power, and the assimilation of the food which has been taken during the day is completed; the system has no need for food immediately after sleep, unless the person went to his rest in a state of starvation. With a system of feeding, which is even a reasonable approach to a natural one, no one can have a real hunger for an early morning breakfast. There is no such thing possible as a normal or genuine hunger immediately after arising from sound sleep. The early morning breakfast is always taken to gratify appetite, never to satisfy hunger. No matter who you are, or what your condition is; no matter how hard you work, or how much you are exposed, unless you go to your bed starved, you cannot arise from your bed hungry.

Hunger is not caused by sleep, but by work. So the best time to eat is when you feel the need for food and not by the clock on the wall.

Physical – What to Eat

What shall I eat? The contests between the vegetarians and the meat eaters, the cooked food advocates, raw food advocates, and various other "schools" of theorists, seem to be interminable; and from the mountains of evidence and argument piled up for and against each special theory, it is plain that if we depend on these scientists we shall never know what we should eat. Turning away from the whole controversy, then, we will ask the question of Mother Nature herself, and we shall find that she has not left us without an answer.

Most of the misinformation and errors of what is a proper dietary grows out of a false premise as to the natural state of a human. When possible, the best source of your daily intake of food right in your area. Local farmers markets, local fish, local dairy and more. Not only does this support the local economy, but you also know the source of your food. By buying local, no need to worry about the questionable growing or shipping practices of food shipped across the globe.

So, I say, the question, "What shall I eat?" has been answered. Eat wheat, corn, oats; eat vegetables; eat meats, eat fruits, eat the things that are eaten by the masses of the people around the world, but purchase them locally.

Also, follow that practice of not eating until you have an earned hunger. This practice will have you craving unnatural, processed or unhealthy foods. For example, when you work in the yard cutting grass and cutting trees from seven in the morning until noon you usually does not come in clamoring for cream puffs and confectioneries. You want more solid food that will replenish both your mind and body.

No matter what your profession, you body will want food that replenishes when you have earned your hunger. When I traveled during my corporate career there were many times while I was in a client's office and was hungry. During these times I simply did what everyone else in the office did and that what to eat a bagel, donut, candy bar and wash it down with a cup of coffee. While my immediate hunger was satisfied, I soon felt irritable as the sugar rush I just ingested began to bring me back to Earth.

As adults it is not necessary to worry about a "varied" diet, so as to get in all the necessary elements. The Chinese and Hindus build very good bodies and excellent brains on a diet of few variations, rice making almost the whole of it. The Scotch are physically and mentally strong on oatmeal cakes; and the Irishman is husky of body and brilliant of mind on potatoes and pork. Form a conception of perfect health for yourself, and do not hold any thought which is not a thought of health.

Follow the practice of never eating until you have an earned hunger. Remember that it will not hurt you in the least to go hungry for a short time; but it will surely hurt you to eat when you are not hungry.

Do not give the least thought to what you should or should not eat; simply eat what is set before you, selecting that which pleases your taste most. In other words, eat what you want within moderation.

Masterminding – Surrounding Yourself with Like-minded People

The coordination of knowledge and effort of two or more people, who work toward a definite purpose, in the spirit of harmony.
~ Napoleon Hill ~

Napoleon Hill formally introduced the "mastermind alliance" in his book entitled "Think and Grow Rich". According to Hill, a mastermind group may be defined as *"the coordination of knowledge and effort of two or more people, who work toward a definite purpose, in the spirit of harmony."* To continue with Hill, "no two minds ever come together without thereby creating a third, invisible intangible force, which may be likened to a third mind [the mastermind itself]."

The Benefits of a Mastermind Group

Now that you have a definition of a mastermind, let's examine the benefits of a mastermind group.

- **Support.** This is vital to your success. That is why I asked you to complete a Family Policy Statement. By surrounding yourself with supportive people, you'll less stress and hassle from the important people in your life. The individuals you involved in your Family Policy Statement may not members of your mastermind group, but it may worth considering inviting them into your group.
- **Resources.** Every person in your group has a different skill set, network of contacts and experience. You never know who knows whom until you ask. These resources could help you success faster.
- **Accountability.** Being a lifestyle entrepreneur, the only person holding your accountable can be a challenge. The members of your group will hold you accountable to your goals.

How to Start a Mastermind Group

Starting a mastermind group is simple.

- **Select your topic.** The specific topic of your mastermind group would be to discuss your lifestyle business. Topics would include niche research, product creation and distribution strategies. One idea to keep in mind is the initial people you invite into your mastermind group may be willing to give their time and effort for free. They may be family members, good friends, etc. Although these individual care about your success, don't expect them to be involved in your group without you providing feedback about their areas if interest. Remember a mastermind is for the benefit of each member of the group. However, since you are putting the group together you can focus on your business first during each meeting.
- **Select your partners.** A mastermind is only as good as the people in it. Select the people involved with care.
- **Limit your group.** Limit the number of your group to 3 to 5 individuals. Any more will usually be unruly and any less may be a challenge to get diverse insight.
- **Meet.** Once you set up your group, schedule one hour weekly meetings. These can be in person or over the phone.

Questions to Ask During Each Meeting

Here are some questions to help structure each meeting.

- What do you need help with?
- What projects or products are you currently working upon?
- What did you achieve since the last meeting?

Time Leverage

You may delay, but time will not.
~ Benjamin Franklin ~

Leveraging your time and that of other will determine how much you get accomplished on a daily basis. Mastering the art of time leverage is critical to your success. It's a combination of time management, multi-tasking and focus. At first glance, that may seem difficult, but after you complete this section and with a little organization you'll realize how simply it really is.

Here are the four components of time leverage you'll learn:
- Time – Yours and that of other people
- Technology – Using technology to achieve more each day
- "Little Black Book". This is your personal resource list. It's where you'll know where to look for what you need when you need it.
- Education – Using up-to-date strategies and techniques will save you time, money and frustration.

Leveraging your time is about organizing your time and activities so you can accomplish multiple tasks in a specific amount of time. In addition, it's about conserving your own energy and resources so you can allocate them to those areas in your life that are most important to you.

When I worked in the corporate world, there were many times that I arrived back home completely exhausted after spending the week on the road. Knowing I only had a few short days to rejuvenate before I had to leave for another week, there many times I completed my weekly call report on Friday evening, not Sunday night like many of the other wholesalers. The call report was my "week-in-review" that I had to submit to my sales manager weekly.

It included all of my activities of the previous week. Once I completed the report I would fax a copy to my manager's home office fax machine. There were many times my manager would call me on Monday morning and say I was "burning myself out" since I was working on Friday night instead of relaxing. However, what my manager didn't know was that I was leveraging my time. You see, every Friday afternoon I asked my internal wholesaler, basically my assistant, to run all of the reports of the previous week and send them to my email account. Prior to getting on the plane to fly home on Friday evening I would download this report and complete it before the plane touched down. Thus, when I arrived home, I simply had to print off the report and fax it to my manager.

The reason I did all of this on Friday was it allowed me to completely forget about work for my entire weekend until I had to leave on Sunday for another grueling week on the road. There were a few times I didn't complete my call report until Sunday evening and for the entire weekend I was stressing about the uncompleted report.

So let's breakdown the how I leveraged my time in the above example:

How I leveraged my time:
- I completed the report while I was flying
- I spent my entire weekend with family and friends not stressing about completing my report on Sunday evening

How I leveraged the time of others:
- My internal wholesaler compiled all of the data I needed to complete my report

How I used technology: (I realize these are very simple ways of using technology)
- I connected with the Internet at the airport to download my reports. Back in the years between 1998 and 2005 the Internet was still very new technology.

Resource list:

- I used the WorldPerks Club, usually at Detroit Metro airport to access the Internet.

How I leveraged my Education:

- I asked my assist to leave a message on my voicemail at the end of very day and answer the following questions:
    - What major events happened in the office today?
    - Any major problems or situations occur today involving any clients?
    - Who is the first person I should talk with tomorrow morning?

As you can see, leveraging your time is about getting more activities out of your time so you can do what you really want to do. In this example, my goal was to completely forget about work for an entire weekend.

Let's learn some proven strategies and techniques you can use to leverage your time. However, before we really get into time leverage strategies and techniques let's learn some basic time management skills.

Time Management – The Very Basic Level

Time management is a skill that can be learned. So don't worry if you feel you currently don't fully manage your time. The best way to look at time management is the creation of new constructive habits and letting go of formerly destructive habits. I learned this while attending a time management seminar while in the corporate world and I have lived by that every since.

Thus is time management is creating new skills, what is time management is not. It is not the need to control your time, but to manage it. Besides, time can't be control any more than the weather, so don't try. The real trick to time management is to be always conscious of the passing of time. When you're conscious of your time, it won't get away from you. The best way to do this is have a goal for each predetermine amount of time. It could be two hours each morning to write a book or an entire Saturday afternoon spending time with friends. It really doesn't matter just have a goal in mind for specific blocks of time. Once you have a goal in mind for each portion of your day, you need to block out time to ensure you achieve that goal each and every day. This blocking of time is called "Power Blocking."

Mastering Your Time

The only asset you have to sell is your time. When you really think about it, how you spend the 1,440 minutes allocated to you everyday determines your lifestyle and your income. There are only two types of tasks you can spend your time on a daily basis. These are busy tasks, while the other is productive tasks.

Here are a few examples of each:

- Busy tasks
  - Spending countless hours watching television
  - Surfing the Internet without a specific goal in mind
  - Reading every email in your inbox
  - Performing non-income or low income producing tasks (doing repetitive tasks you can outsource to others)

- Productive Tasks
  - Spending quality time with family and friends
  - Taking courses or attending webinars to improve your skills
  - Listening to business-related audio programs, instead of the radio, while driving
  - Make the decision that everything you do in life brings you closer to your lifetime goals

Let's take a look at the "Productivity Pyramid". The Productivity Pyramid is a visual representation of how to allocate your time to ensure you are only focusing on the most productive activities during your working hours. The most productive activities are those that create an income for your business. The only activities that I know of that actually create actual cash is when you make a sale. Here is a visual representation of the pyramid for my business.

As you can see, the most productive and profitable time is when I am actually closing sales and selling my products. The second most productive is the time spent during the "Must Be Done" hours. This is the time you must spend to create your products to sell or preparing for a webinar or teleseminar. This is your preparation time. Without creating new products or preparing for webinars, you'll never have something to sell. Finally, the wasted hours is time spent doing thing that has nothing to do with actually creating an income for my lifestyle business. Unfortunately, many people spend most of their time near the bottom of the pyramid doing low productivity activities and wonder why their business isn't succeeding and their lifestyle isn't what they want it to be.

You need to "move your time up the pyramid" so that you are allocating more time doing activities near the top of the pyramid. Thus, each day you are doing more productive and high value activities.

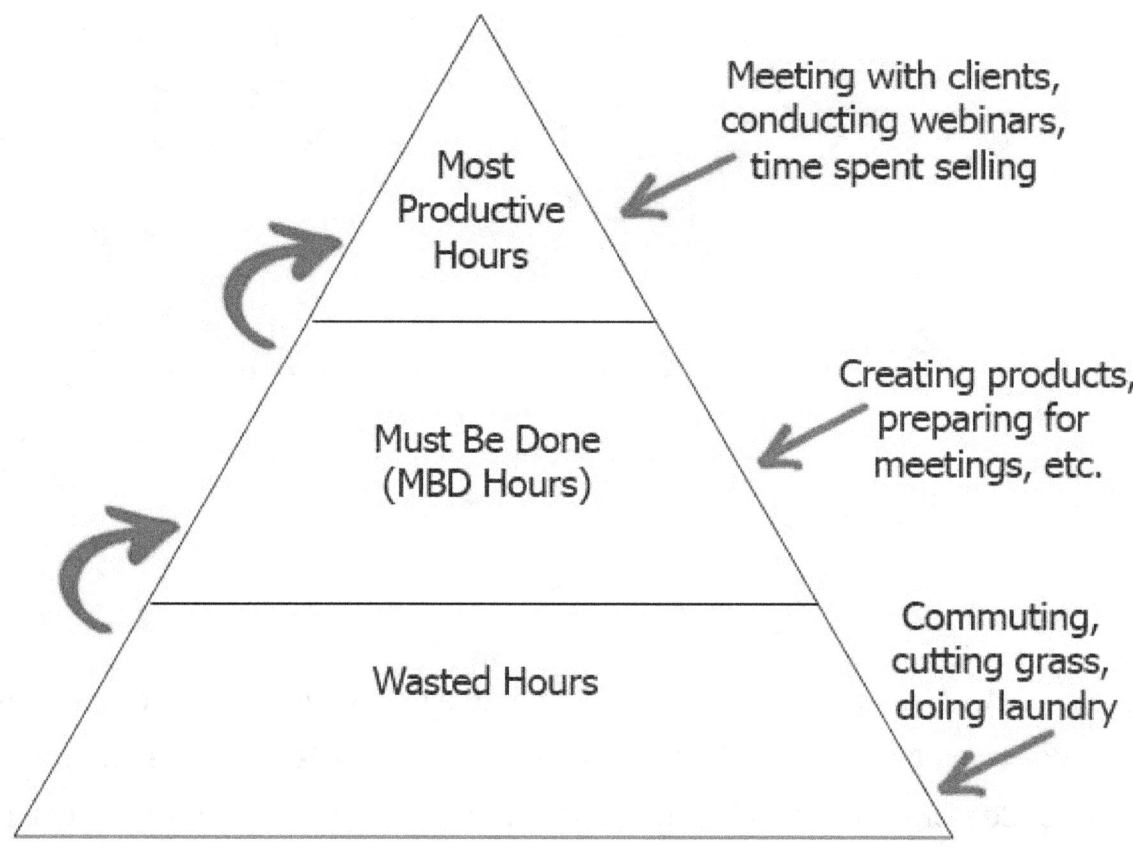

The ultimate goal is to completely invert your Productivity Pyramid so you can spend your entire day on high-value activities only. The only way to achieve your lifestyle goals is to leverage your time. For example, in the corporate world you trade one hour of your time for your hourly wage. That is a 1-to-1 ratio. Being a lifestyle entrepreneur you need to increase that ratio to 25 to 100 and 1000 to one. That is why you need to invert your time and focus. Focus only the activities that will get you closer to your goals.

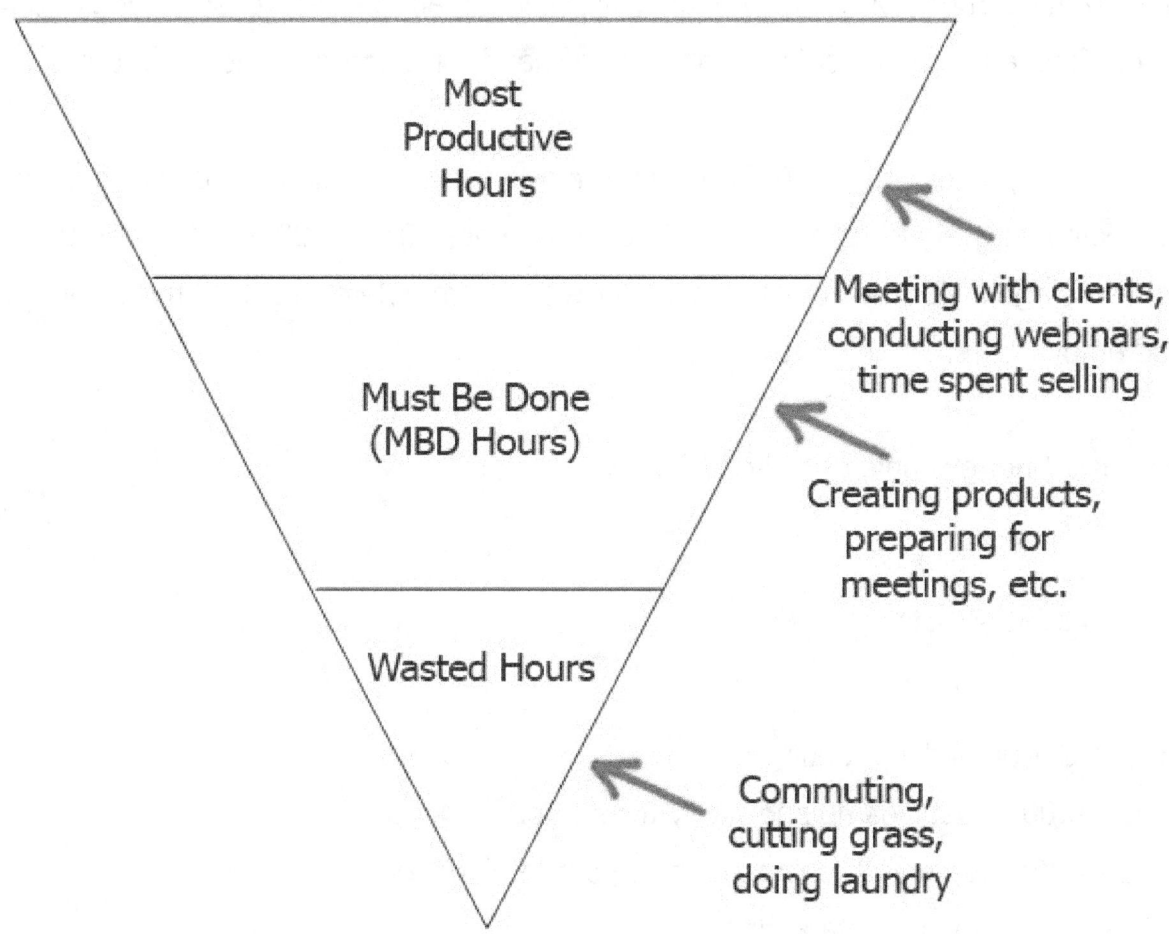

So what is the best way to ensure you'll be always performing productive tasks even when you are relaxing? One of the best ways to do this is to follow a strategy called "Power Blocking" I first learned this strategy from an experienced real estate agent a few days after I earned my real estate license when I was 18 years old. I have used it ever since in all aspects of my life. I used it in my real estate career, while I attended college, as a mutual fund wholesaler and now as a lifestyle entrepreneur.

Power blocking is a way to have a high productive daily schedule. It is when you block out 45 minutes of each hour of the day for a dedicated task with the remaining 15 minutes for taking a break. For example, spend 9:00 – 9:45 a.m. reading and responding to emails and then the final 15 minutes in the 9 o'clock hour taking a quick walk to the corner store. This productivity management strategy ensures you're always highly focused in the most important task at hand for a specific amount of time.

The first step in getting started is to determine how you spend each day of the week. For example, every Sunday evening I spend one hour from 5:00 to 6:00 p.m. to review my goals for the coming week. Once this is complete I turn off the computer and enjoy the remainder of the evening.

Here is a brief example of daily schedule.

Daily Activity List:

6:00: - Get up and work out

7:00 – 8:00: - Get kids up and ready for school

8:00 –9:30: - Read and reply to emails, post to blogs, etc.

9:30 – 11:00: - Online Marketing

11:00 – 12:30: - Eat lunch

12:30 – 1:00: - Return telephone messages and check email

1:00 – 2:00: - Affiliate Marketing

2:00 – 3:00: - Offline Marketing

3:00 – 4:00: - Review emails, return telephone calls, respond to emails

4:00 – 6:00: - Get ready for dinner, spend time with family

6:00 – 9:00: - Product Creation Session

Now that you have learned how to manage your time by having a goal for each hour of the day and then setting dividing your day into "power blocks", the next step is to learn how to leverage your time and other people's time.

Leveraging Your Time

At its core, leveraging your time is having the mindset that every task you do (*accomplish multiple tasks in a specific amount of time*) can be used multiple times (*conserving your own energy and resources so you can allocate them to those areas in your life that are most important to you*). There are two vital steps in leveraging your time for maximum benefits:

1. Determine what exactly you want to leverage.
2. Determine how to leverage your output.

Let me explain, before you can leverage your time you need to determine exactly what needs to be accomplished and then how you can leverage it.

For example, you are responsible for performing the sales and marketing for your company. This includes writing articles, press releases, closing sales, etc.

What needs to be accomplished?

1. Writing a 250 word daily blog post

How can this be leveraged?

1. Post to your blog
2. Convert to an audio file and post on your blog
3. Convert to a video and post to YouTube

Using the example above, you have just leveraged your time for maximum benefits. You have taken the 250 word blog post and converted it into an audio and a video file. For a few extra minutes of work of converting your blog post, you now have three different ways of sharing the same message with your customers and potential customers.

Here is how you can convert your written post into an audio and then a video

- **Step #1:** Download the free, open source software called Audacity. This is an excellent tool for recording and editing audio. www.audacity.com
- **Step #2:** Record yourself reading your blog post. You have just created an MP3 audio of your blog post.
  - **Step #2A:** If you don't want to record your blogpost in your own voice, check out Odiogo.com www.odiogo.com This is a text-to-audio service that converts your blogposts into a podcast. This is achieved by using a near human speaking software. You simply place a line of code in your site and the service converts is automatically to be place directly on your site.
- **Step #3:** Sign up for the free video creation service called Animoto. www.animoto.com This free service allows you to create slide show videos. Used the audio from step two as the background audio for your slide show video.

In less than 20 minutes you have created two additional products (audio and video) from a single blog post and best of all it was free to create. The next step is distribution. The free service called PixelPipe www.pixelpipe.com will distribute all types of files to multiple online destinations with a single click of a button.

By following the example above you have just leveraged a single blog post into multiple products and distributed those products to multiple locations. The primary purpose of implementing time leveraging strategies is to give you the free time so you can enjoy your personal life.

Time Leverage Worksheet

Use the worksheet below determine what activities in your business you do on daily basis that can be leveraged:

What needs to be accomplished? _____

How can this be leveraged? _____

_____

What needs to be accomplished? _____

How can this be leveraged? _____

_____

What needs to be accomplished? _____

How can this be leveraged? _____

_____

What needs to be accomplished? _____

How can this be leveraged? _____

_____

Here are additional strategies you can use to leverage your time.

1. Social Media. Link all of your social media sites together. For example, did you know if you are using a Wordpress blog, each post can be linked to your twitter and Facebook account. This means you are writing your post once and all of the other linked accounts will be updated, also. Here is a list of some of the resources you can use to link your social media sites together:
   - Wordpress:
     - http://wordpress.org/extend/plugins/
   - Twitter:
     - HootSuite - www.hootsuite.com
     - NetVibes - www.netvibes.com
   - LinkedIn:
     - LinkedIn for Outlook 2010 – In your Outlook email
   - Facebook:
     - Facebook Connect – www.facebook.com
   - Google Plus+
     - Google Plus+ - www.google.com

2. Have an operations manual. This is a manual this outlines and details all of your practices and systems. The benefit of having an operations manual is it will keep you on track. It helps you to understand each part of your business.

3. Have an employee handbook. Even if you don't have employees, write an employee handbook for yourself. It can be only a few pages long, but just like an operations manual it helps you to understand what is expected from yourself and your employees.

4. Automate your business. Use contact management services like Aweber www.Aweber.com and Constant Contact www.constantcontact.com These are excellent services you can use to create one email and send out to your customer base. In addition, use Quickbooks for your bookkeeping.

Leveraging Your Time for Product Creation

You can also use this strategy to help you create new types of products and services you can sell in your business, too. Remember, the core concept of leveraging your time is to create it once for multiple outputs.

This strategy can be used in any type of industry. Always look for leverage in the products you create. For example, if you are a food company the time spent to create your recipe (input) is used multiple times when you mass produce your product (output). You created your recipe once, yet your business produces 5,000 jar's a day of the same recipe.

Here are a few examples of different business models and how each business can leverage its initial output of the products created or skills learned.

Industry	Initial time input	Leverage
Food Business	Create the recipe once	Mass produce the recipe
Coaching business	Write a book	Conduct a seminar Create a membership program
Health Related Business	Learn the skills to become a yoga instructor	Conduct online webinars
Heating and Cooling Business	Learn the skills to repair furnaces and air conditioners	Create how-to videos for minor maintenance

As you can see from the few examples above any type of business can create leveraged products or services from what they are already doing.

Leveraging the Time of Others

Money Loves Speed

~ Original Author Unknown ~

Your Five Day Weekend business has a number of different components that must be addressed on a daily basis, however this doesn't mean you are doing all of the work. These include:

- Traffic generation
- Link building
- Order fulfillment
- Product creation
- List building and more.

You have two choices to business online. You can try to do everything yourself or you can leverage the time of other people. In a word, you outsource. Leveraging the time of others is outsourcing activities to competent individuals who can get more done is less time at a fair price. The more you outsource, the faster your business can grow since your focusing your time on growing your business.

Outsourcing is vital to the success of your lifestyle business. However, many find it difficult to find the right people at the right price that you can partner with to grow your business. However, before you decide what parts of your business you want to outsource, you need to decide what you are good at and want to do. As your business grows, you'll be able to outsource more and more of your activities however in the beginning you'll need decide what you want to do in-house.

At this point I realize everyone reading this material has different lifestyle goals, experiences, located in different parts of the globe and interested in different niches. However, the one common thread is the Internet will be vital to the growth of your business. It doesn't matter what niche you are in or if you have a physical product (food, car parts, etc.), a service business (personal coaching) or a digital business (ebooks, membership sites, etc.). Your business will be using the Internet. To build a lifestyle business, you'll need to incorporate as much Internet marketing and outsourcing strategies as possible. So with that as the thread, we'll focus on the different parts of your business and what areas are needed.

There are five components for any lifestyle business.

1. Traffic Generation – Getting people to your site
2. Conversions – Getting individuals to buy
3. Product Creation – What are you selling
4. Order fulfillment – Get your product into your customers hands
5. Technology – Internet and websites

So take a look at the general list and decide what you like to do. The best way to do this is to prioritize the list. For example, if you like creating new products for your niche, but are terrible at technical stuff, you'll be focusing all of your time on product creation and outsourcing everything else. Use the worksheet below to prioritize your talents, skills and abilities.

1. _____
2. _____
3. _____
4. _____
5. _____

By completing the above exercise, you not only discover what you will be outsourcing for your business, but this very same list gives you insight to what other people will pay you to do. If you hate technology (creating websites), but are good at copyrighting (conversion) you can create a lifestyle business offering copyright services to others.

Let's turn our attention to place you can go to outsource, also called virtual assistances and maybe even offer your services for sale to other lifestyle entrepreneurs.

- Fiverr – www.fiverr.com
- oDesk – www.odesk.com
- Guru – www.guru.com
- Freelancer – www.freelancer.com
- Getafreelancer – www.getafreelancer.com

These sites are ideal for finding freelancers, virtual assistances and more. Use these resources to for the following areas of your business:

1. Traffic Generation – Getting people to your site
2. Conversions – Getting individuals to buy
3. Product Creation – What are you selling
4. Technology – Internet and websites

One of the only areas of your business that you probably won't any assistance for on the sites listed above is order fulfillment. Fulfillment companies will store and ship your products to your customers allowing you to never have to worry about touching any of your products, they will do it all for you. Here is a list of order fulfillment companies for physical products:

Leveraging your Time - Leveraging Technology

Technology can do amazing things for you and your business. Leveraging technology is both an art and a science. It's an art when you design systems to help you get more out of your business. It's a science when you apply those technologies. However, just become you can do something really cool with technology should you do it?

When leveraging technology you need to keep in mind three vital questions.

- What do you want to do accomplish with it?
- Why are you doing it?
- Is your communication personal?

Before you implement a new technology in your personal life or business, ask yourself those three questions. For example, you enjoy operating your business on your laptop from a poolside cabana. While the advantages are obvious, here are some of the pitfalls of running your business next to the pool.

- No access to other vital office equipment. ie, fax machine, all of your audio equipment to record audios, etc.
- Talk to your domestic and International customer and suppliers from your computer for free.
- Unable to share vital documents with your suppliers and partners.

Here is the solution to those issues by leverage technology:

- Convert your PDF's to fax and use the following services:
    - Efax – www.efax.com
    - Fax – www.fax.com
    - Myfax – www.myfax.com
- Use the following services to record audio:
    - Google Voice – www.google.com This is a free service offers a number of excellent services including voice recording, message service, transcribe your messages and more.
    - Dragon Naturally Speaking - www.nuance.com/dragon/index.htm This is excellent software voice recognition software. Basically, you speak and it types. This is create for capturing ideas and creating products without typing.
- Check out these services that you can make call over the Internet
    - Skype – www.skype.com
    - Humnut – www.humnut.com
- Use these services to share documents online with your partners and suppliers, etc.
    - Google Docs www.docs.google.com
    - 4shared – www.4shared.com

As you can see from the above example the answer the first two questions are:

- What do you want to do accomplish with it?
  - Answer: Operate my business at the same level of professionalism and quality as if I was in my office
- Why are you doing it?
  - Answer: So I can have the complete freedom of running my business from any location on the globe.
- Are you keeping your communication personal?
  - Answer: See below

Technology does have its downfall and that is its inability to provide the personal touch. Without a personal touch strategy for your business all of your technology strategies will fail.

You must have a personal touch strategy in place for all of your communications. This is as simple as knowing what your customers what and delivering it to them. It doesn't have to be complicated. Here is how to do it leverage technology:

Knowing what you customers what can be easily determined by asking them to complete a simply online survey. You can use a free service called Survey Monkey www.surveymonkey.com By using this service you can create a 10 question survey and collect the data via your website, email or Facebook. Once you have the results of what your customers want to the next step is to provide them with the product. You can even find out how they want your products or services delivered by asking them questions in your survey. Surveys are an excellent way to provide a personal touch while leveraging technology.

So let's take a closer look at how you can leverage technology to enjoy five day weekends. While I'm not going to go into the very basic stuff of buying a domain name and setting up your webhosting, instead in this section I am going to provide a list of some of the technology I use to maximize productivity.

As you know if you want to do business on the Internet you need a domain and hosting account. Check out these services:

- Godaddy – www.godaddy.com
- Register.com – www.register.com
- Network Solutions – www.networksolutions.com
- Host Gator – www.hostgator.com

Now that you have your domain and hosting the next level of technology leveraging is the framework of your site. Thanks to free, open source content management systems (CMS) you can set up and design your own site for zero cost. It's almost as easy as a "just as water" recipe. In fact, most of the hosting companies offer one-click installations as part of their low cost services. Here are some of the benefits of CMS available today:

- Ability to manage your website and content without a webmaster or programming skills.
- They are completely scalable
- They are free
- They are easy to design
- Internet security is provided by the hosting company for your hosting account

Here are some of the more popular CMS systems:

- WordPress
- Drupal
- Joomla

Now that you have your site set you and the next area is to leverage is the communication with your customers. The mains areas of communication to your customers is from your website and your email communications. Here are some areas to leverage for each.

If you are using a CMS-based website (WordPress, etc.), use third party extensions to connect your website with all of your other social accounts. Check out WordPress www.wordpress.org to learn more. The reason I am not going to provide examples is technology is this area moves to fast and the minute I create a list of excellent plugins many of them would be out-of-date.

Check out these email tools to help you leverage your business:

Aweber – www.aweber.com

Constant Contact – www.constantcontact.com

Icontact – www.icontact.com

Vertical Response – www.verticalresponse.com

The next area is your social network. While a complete and detailed explanation of each of the social marketing sites is outside the scope book, you can check out our website www.FiveDayWeekend.com for a more detailed explanation of each of the network. However, for the purposes of this book, I'll focus on how to use each in your lifestyle business.

Many individuals know they must use social marketing in their lifestyle businesses, but they aren't sure exactly what is it and how to get the most out of it. However, before we go any further, let's define the term social media. According to Wikipedia social media is defined as,

"Social media includes web-based and mobile technologies used to turn communication into interactive dialogue."

Not that we have a definition, before you leverage social marketing of your lifestyle business, you first need to why WHY you are going to focus on social media. You have to have a purpose and know what you what. The greatest benefit of social media is it's all about the customer. It's the personal touch your business needs.

One of the best ways to start a social media strategy for your business is to take some time and decide what you want out of it. Here are four reasons to use social media:

- Personal Use – Entertainment and connecting with family, friends, etc.
- Business – Communication with new and existing customers
- Business – Networking with other professionals
- Marketing – Generation new customers and up-selling existing customers

Here is a list of the different forms of social media that exist with websites:

- Blogging
    - Wordpress
    - Blogger
    - Typepress
- Forums
    - Yahoo Answers
- Microblogging
    - Twitter
    - Jaiku
    - Tumblr
- Social Networking
    - Facebook
    - LinkedIn
    - MySpace
    - MeetUp
- Video Sharing
    - YouTube
    - MetaCafe
    - Daily Motion

We now have a list of four main reasons why you use social media and a list of some of the different forms of social media. Let's now bring everything together into a strategy you can use for your lifestyle business. While every social media site has the ability to be used for both personal use and business, I'll break it down which sites I spend most of my time for business and personal use. Also, keep in mind communication strategies and marketing strategies are two completely different approaches, too. Implementing a communication strategy is a less direct type of communication then a pure sales and marketing message. Simply use this list as a building block for your lifestyle business.

- Personal Use Sites – These are some sites to use for entertainment and personal interaction with friends, family, etc.
    - Facebook
    - YouTube
- Business – Connecting with new and existing customers
    - Twitter
    - Facebook
    - Yahoo Answers
- Business – Networking with other professionals
    - LinkedIn
    - MeetUp
- Marketing - Generation new customers and up-selling existing customers
    - Facebook
    - YouTube
    - Twitter

The next step is to decide what you want to accomplish with your social media marketing and which platforms you'll use. For example, your lifestyle business helps others to create and market food recipes. Here is an example of your social media strategy:

- What is the purpose of my social media strategy?:
    - Marketing - To generate new customers
- Which platforms will I use?:
    - Facebook
- What will I provide?:
    - Facebook – I will post a how-to video with link to my site
- How am I keeping it personal?:
    - Facebook - I will provide video tips on starting a food business

Use the worksheet below to create your social media marketing strategy.

What is the purpose of my social media strategy?:

_____

_____

_____

_____

Which platforms will I use?:

_____

_____

_____

_____

What will I provide?:

_____

_____

_____

_____

How am I keeping it personal?:

_____

_____

_____

_____

Leveraging your Time - Little Black Book – Your Personal Resource List

Keeping everything organized and accessible is vital to the success of your lifestyle business. Since you'll have to access your information from many different locations, you want to store your information online. Check out the resources in this section to keep everything together.

I still remember the huge clunk sound I heard while I was in Nashville, Tennessee when I worked in the corporate world. I returned to into my rental car after lunch meeting and was on the way to my next meeting. There must be something magical about hitting 35 miles per hour with a laptop on the roof of your car. That is the exact wind velocity that will force the computer that was forgotten on the roof of the car to bounce off the trunk and finally smash it on the road. I caught a glimpse of the corner my computer sliding off the trunk after I looked into the rearview mirror when I heard the initial clunk sound. Fortunately, all of my files were synced up with my assistants computer only a few hours before. However, this can devastating if you are operating your lifestyle business half way across the country.

In this section, you'll learn to have access to all of your information without the worry of losing it if something happens to your computer. These can be used while you are either in your office or not. We'll rely on web-based apps including document sharing tools, calendars, password software, virtual offices and more.

For many, sending a receiving mail and packages is vital to your business. Check out these services for mail and packages:

- Earth Class Mail – www.earthclassmail.com
- Virtual Post Mail – www.virtualpostmail.com

The next area you'll need to set up is a place to store all of your passwords online. It is said that the only things that are certain in life is death and taxes. However, with the creation of the Internet the third certainty is life is you are certain to lose your passwords. Check out the following online services to keep your passwords safe and accessible.

- PassPack - www.passpack.com
- RoboForm - www.roboform.com

Collaboration, virtual office, calendars and document sharing is another area your need. Fortunately, with cloud-based technology, you don't need to have a bunch of programs on your computer any more. These services can turn your browser into a complete office suite including document sharing, word processor, project management, spreadsheet and more.

- Drop Box – www.dropbox.com Used for document sharing, presentations and more
- Zoho Office – www.zoho.com This site offers a complete array of services from email, web conferencing, project management and more.
- Google Calendar – www.google.com/calender Keep your calendar online. You can also allow others to access your calendar too.

Check out these online contact management services to keep in contact with everyone you need to reach.

- Funclient – www.funclient.com
- Highrisehq – www.highrisehq.com

Another area that you need to incorporate in your business is virtual meetings. You can having meeting without leaving your desk. Many of these services do require a month cost but some remaining free.

- GoToMeeting – www.gotomeeting.com
- WebEx – www.webex.com
- Vyew – www.vyew.com – Free meeting software

Leveraging Your Education

Leveraging your education is a combination of proper time management, having the right resources and the implementation of the plan. Keeping up-to-date in your industry and the latest marketing strategy will keep you head of your competitors.

Traveling 150 nights per year in the corporate has taught me numerous ways to upgrade my education while on the road and at home. The key to maintaining your education while is to have the right tools to use while you're traveling. For example, I also my mobile phone has hours of MP3's stored on it. Rather than listening to the radio while I'm on the road, I connect my mobile phone to my car stereo.

In addition to listening to audios while I drive, I attended a speed reading course. This skill alone will help increase your income since it'll take you less time to read the material.

Here are some of the best ways to leverage your education while at home or on the road.

- Listen to educational MP3's in your car and airplanes.
  - You car can be a "university on wheels". If you spend just 10 hours per week in your car, that's 500 hours per year learning.
- Buy a Kindle and read ebooks while traveling.
  - No sense carrying around your laptop while traveling when you can read all of your ebooks on a Kindle.
- Attend to live teleseminars while in your car.
  - Simply dial into the teleseminar, plug in your mobile phone to the car speakers and listen to the call.
- Attend at least one webinar in your niche weekly
  - A few hours attending a webinar can keeps you up-to-date with cutting edge strategies
- Power block at least two hours each week to read blogs in your niche
  - Only ready two or three high quality blogs and RSS feeds, etc. There are simply too many new websites popping up every day to follow. Find a few that you like and read them only.
- Attend an internet marketing seminar in your niche once a quarter
  - When you attend a live event you not only learn great information, you also meet other people in your industry. These individuals could make great partners or members of your mastermind group.
- "Rip-n-read" I learned the "rip-n-read" approach from one of my national sales managers in the corporate world.
  - Instead of reading every page of a magazine, simply flip through the magazine for interesting articles and "rip them out." Keep these in a file and read them while you're on the plane or on the beach.
- Only follow two or three guru's

- o It seems everywhere you look online, everyone is a self-proclaimed expert. However, you soon realize many of these "experts" are people who never really succeeded in what they are teaching. Find two or three guru's to follow and forget the rest.

Income Leverage

Making money from your lifestyle business is the only true measure of the quality, performance and customer acceptance of your product. You can have the best marketing plan, the best looking website and the best product at the lowest price, but if you are not building your list and making money, you won't be able to live the lifestyle you want and deserve. Not to say that a lifestyle business is all about the money, but the reality is if you don't have money to support your lifestyle, you don't have a lifestyle. So how can you ensure that your lifestyle business will always be building you a list and making money? The answer is to "Add Value" to your customers.

The term "add value" is an ambiguous and widely overused term. However, you must add value before anyone will purchase your product or service. So how can you add value to your customers? The best way to add value is to ensure that you are providing a product or service that enhances their life or business with every communication they receive from your company. You must invest your time and energy in being genuine help to your customers. When your customers see they just received an email from your company, you'll genuinely be able to say "They always know I only send great information to help them loss weight. Or, they always know I have great ideas to help them grow their business." Providing genuine help with every communication is the only way to add value to your customers.

You simply don't offer them a product or service, you offer them your expertise, your experience and your insight to help them improve their lives or grow their business. In three words, you are "genuine adding value" to help them achieve a specific goal. You must add value for people to subscribe to your email list or purchase your product. Now that we understand we must add genuine value to our customers, let's turn our attention to creating the type of products to offer.

Income Leverage – Product Creditability:

At this point, some people may not feel they have the creditability or the experience that others will pay to learn. What is great about life is each of us has unique and different experiences and those experiences make us who we are today. What we take for granted, others will gladly pay for since our experience is helping them to achieve their goals and dreams.

In addition to creating an entire array of products based upon your unique experience and insight, you can also interview experts. This is an excellent option since you can leverage the creditability and experience of others to build your business. For example, let's say you want launch a business in the mortgage niche, but you don't have any experience in finance or mortgage. You would interview a number of mortgage bankers about what to look for in a mortgage company and how to negotiate the best rate and terms. The next step would be turn these interviews into an eBook, audios and even a video series and sell them from your website.

The greatest benefit to interviewing experts is you instantly become the expert in your selected niche. In addition, these same individuals you interviewed to create your product will be the same group that could also become joint venture partners to help you sell your product. They would also be promoting this product to their list of customers, thus leveraging distribution and increasing sales.

Income Leverage – Niche Research:

I am a firm believer in offering a complete array of different product types to my customers. These include a strategic combination of both physical and digital products. Here are few examples of each product type:

- Physical Products:
  - Food products – jam, jellies, salsa, syrup etc.
  - Dietary supplements
  - Electronics
  - Clothes, etc.
- Digital Products:
  - Ebooks
  - Videos
  - Audios
  - Personal coaching, etc.

While my companies offer both physical and digital products, for the remainder of this material I will go into detail about the leveraging digital products as the product of choice for your lifestyle business. The reason is digital products provide the greatest amount of flexibility, ease of creation, fulfillment and profitability. Physical products have an additional level of consideration including manufacturing, shipping logistics and more that is simply beyond the scope of this material. However, we do offer a complete coaching course on physical products at www.fivedayweekend.com

However, even when you have physical products, you still need to offer an entire array of digital products to help market and support your physical product line to achieve maximum profitability.

The very first step in product creation is deciding what you love to do? In the Lifestyle Leverage you completed the *What is my true passion? – What type of work do I really love? Worksheet* use the answers will help you to determine what basic type of market niche you should be in.

However, before we go any further, let's define what exactly is a market niche. According to Wikipedia.com the definition of a market niche is:

*"A **niche market** is the subset of the market on which a specific product is focusing; therefore the market niche defines the specific product features aimed at satisfying specific market needs, as well as the price range, production quality and the demographics that is intended to impact."*

The next step is to look at your answers from a realistic point of view. While passion for what you do is an important factor to your success, you need to consider the profit potential. For example, if you are passionate about "growing butternut squash" it would be difficult for this mirco-niche to support your lifestyle business. A better approach would to compromise a bit and build a business around "gardening". You could create educational products about best gardening tips with a chapter on "growing butternut squash". In addition, you write a book and create videos on how to grow and crave the best Halloween pumpkins. In fact, many national televisions seek "experts" to talk about Halloween decorations during the month of October.

If you're still not sure on what type of niche market you should be, check out this list of most profitable online niches.

1. Health – Diet, exercise, weight loss, how to look better (sexy), etc.
2. Money – Make money, home business, business success, etc.
3. Relationships – family relationships, dating, personal interaction and communication

If you're still stumped about what niche you should be in for your business, the next strategy is to consider the highest cost per click in Google AdWords. The amount a company is willing to pay for a single click has a direct relation to how much they expect to earn from that click/customer. That is why the most expensive AdWords can also provide insight to the most profitable online niches. One of the leading providers of software for keyword and pay-per-click marketing campaigns is WordStream. The company has conducted some research on which keywords receive the highest cost per click (CPC) in Google AdWords.

Check out this partial list compiled near the end of 2011.

1. *Insurance* - $54.91 per click (example, "buy car insurance online")
2. *Loans* - $44.28 per click (example, "student loans")
3. *Mortgage* - $47.12 per click (example, "refinance second mortgages")
4. *Attorney* - $47.07 per click (example, "personal injury attorney")
5. *Credit* - $36.06 per click (example, "home equity line of credit")
6. *Lawyer* - $42.51 per click (example, "personal injury lawyer")
7. *Donate* - $42.02 per click (example, "donating a used car")
8. *Degree* - $40.61 per click (example, "criminal justice degrees online")

To learn more about their services check out their website. www.wordstream.com

Income Leverage – Product Creation:

We already discussed two strategies to create products including:

1. Created from your own experience
2. Interview experts and sell the transcripts

Here are additional two options you can use to help jump your product creation. These include private label rights (PLR) and public domain (PD) options. While these options aren't usually the highest quality they can provide you with an starting block for rapid product creation. When using PLR and PD information, you'll always want to make the information and content authentic. This means don't simply just cut-n-paste this information and use it as it.

Here is a brief definition of PLR and PD as defined by Wikipedia.com:

Private Label Rights:

"Private label rights is a concept used in Internet Marketing and derived from private labeling. It's a license where the author sells most or all of the intellectual property rights to their work."

Public Domain:

*"Works are in the **public domain** if the intellectual property rights have expired, if the intellectual property rights are forfeited, or if they are not covered or protected by intellectual property laws."*

Both PLR and PD information is best used as a resource and not the main content for your material. The disadvantage of both PLR and PD is that many other people may be using the exact information in their business and marketing strategies. The best way to use these resources is to edit the material and make it your own by placing your own personality and voice into it.

Now that you have selected a niche, created a product what are the different ways you can offer that material to your customers so you can not only leverage your material but also add genuine value to your customers.

However, before you simply go out and create different variations of your material you need to understand the value they add to your customers and how each variation leverages your income. I call these different variations "value-added communication". Because with each type of communication your customers are getting more value to help improve their life and your business get value since you are leveraging your income:

- Email communication:
    - Value to the customer: Receive brief insight and tips
        - Cost: Free
    - Value to your business: Builds your list
        - Estimate cost to produce: Free
- Print Newsletter:
    - Value to the customer: In-depth articles
        - Cost: $10 - $25 for monthly subscription fee
    - Value to your business: Builds your list and can charge monthly subscription fee
        - Estimate cost to produce: Usually low printing and shipping fees

- Ebook:
  - Value to the customer: In-depth information
    - Cost: Free - $15
  - Value to your business: Builds your list, positions you as the expert and income source
    - Estimate cost to produce: Free or low cost if you hire a freelancer to write
- Audio/Video:
  - Value to the customer: In-depth information and different of learning your material
    - Cost: Free - $25
  - Value to your business: Builds your list, positions you as the expert and income source
    - Estimate cost to produce: Free or low cost if you hire a freelancer for the voice over
- Membership Site:
  - Value to the customer: In-depth training
    - Cost: $25 - $97 per month
  - Value to your business: Recurring and leverage income stream for your business
    - Estimate cost to produce: Purchase membership tracking software - $100 - $300
- Group Coaching (Webinar or Teleseminar):
  - Value to the customer: In-depth and some personalized information
    - Cost: $49 - $297 per month
  - Value to your business: Positions you as the expert and leveraged income source for your business
    - Estimate cost to produce: Monthly cost of $50 - $100

- Boot Camps
  - Value to the customer: In-depth and some personalized information
    - Cost: $295 - $995 One-time cost
  - Value to your business: Positions you as the expert and leveraged income source for your business
    - Estimate cost to produce: Varies
- One-on-One Coaching and Consulting
  - Value to the customer: Very in-depth and very personalized
    - Cost: $1,250 - $2,500 (could be one time or monthly)
  - Value to your business: Positions you as the expert and leveraged income source for your business
    - Estimate cost to produce: Varies – However, usually very low since this can be accomplished over the phone

Now let's turn our focus to using technology to increase your profit margin to your business and adding genuine value to your customers.

You can also choose to have physical products to sell. Here are a few additional components you need to consider when you have a physical:

- Who will manufacture your physical?
- Where will you store your product?
- Who will ship your product to your customers?

Here are a few resources to get you started with finding manufacturers and products

- Alibaba – www.alibaba.com You can find almost any type of product from manufactures across the globe. No matter what your niche you can find a product to sell. From electronics to foods to auto parts. If you can't find a source here, it probably isn't made.
- Thomas Register of Manufacturers – www.thomasnet.com A listing of every possible manufacturer for every conceivable product.
- Tech Data – www.techdata.com Electronic related manufacturers.

Additional strategies to find physical products for your business.

Attend tradeshows. Tradeshows are ideal to find products you can private label or resell in your business. No matter what niche you are in you can walk the floor of a tradeshow and discover products you never knew existed. Check out the list below to help get you started:

- Vitamins and Consumables
    - ExpoEast – www.expoeast.com
    - ExpoWest – www.expowest.com – I have attended both ExpoEast and ExpoWest with excellent success
    - PLMI (Private Label Trade Show) - www.groceryheadquarters.com
- Hardware and Housewares
    - National Hardware Show – www.nationalhardwareshow.com
    - International Housewares Association - www.housewares.org/
- Calendars of All Different Types of Tradeshows
    - Trade Shows for Importers of China and Asia-Made Products - http://tradeshowcalendar.globalsources.com
    - Events in America - http://www.eventsinamerica.com

Income Leverage – Creating your System to Leverage Technology:

The technology to operate your lifestyle is simply amazing. Unlike 15 years ago when almost everything surrounding the Internet was clunky and cumbersome you can now have a website up and running in less than 20 minutes. It's simply amazing. It's much easier to get started, but that doesn't mean you'll be successful. To succeed you need to create a system for both website creation and follow up with your prospects and customers.

A system is your operations manuals for each part of your business. It is a complete step-by-step guide you follow to achieve a specific goal. The more detailed your system the better it is for your business. When creating your system, write down every step in great detail. The reason you need to create a system for every part of your business is so you can give this manual to your virtual assistants and they can run your business while you are enjoying your lifestyle.

For example, your goal is to diversify your business income by entering into a new niche. Here is a brief example of the system you could follow:

Product Creation System

1. Look at the hobbies and activities you like to do and do some market research to see if people are spending for products and services in this niche.
2. Visit forums and blogs and see what people are talking about.
3. Conduct niche research
   a. Use Google Keyword Tool - https://adwords.google.com/select/KeywordToolExternal
   b. Quancast – www.quantcast.com Find out the number of monthly visitors for most websites. You also get an insight on the what keywords generated the inbound traffic to the website

    c. Spyfu – www.spyfu.com Discover what your competitors keywords, what they are spending per month for online advertising and more.

4. Decide on the type of you free product you want to create and give away to build your list
   a. Ebook
   b. Video
   c. Audio

5. Who will create the content for your product
   a. Hire a freelancer to write content from Guru – www.guru.com
   b. Edit private label rights material and as a resource chapter
   c. Will you create the product yourself

6. Create a squeeze page to give away your free report to build your list

7. Create buzz for your new product
   a. Facebook page
   b. Twitter account
   c. YouTube channel

8. Send survey to your list to see what type of product they are willing to pay for.
   a. Survey Monkey – www.surveymonkey.com
   b. AYTM – www.aytm.com You can conduct your very own market research using AYTM and use the results to create your ideal product.

9. Create the actual product you are going to be selling from the survey results in #8.

10. Create the website that will sell your actual digital product.

11. Set up an affiliate program for your new product
    a. Clickbank – www.clickbank.com
    b. CommissionJunction (CJ) – www.cj.com

12. Create an audio from the ebook
    a. Use Audacity to make recording – www.audacity.com
    b. Or Hire an individual from Guru.com for voiceover

13. Create a sales video

    a. Use Animoto – www.animoto.com

    b. Use Camtasia – www.camtasia.com

14. Create the products you'll sell on the backend

    a. OTO's – One time Offers

    b. Monthly memberships

    c. Downsells

Website Creation System

1. Purchase domain

    a. Register.com – www.register.com

2. Purchase Hosting

    a. Hostgator.com – www.hostgator.com

3. Create a blog site using Wordpress

    a. Installed on the hosting account

    b. Install plugins (Since plugins are always being introduced, I'm not going to include a list here, however visit www.FiveDayWeekend.com for a list of must have, up-to-date plugins)

4. Install lead capture form

    a. Install email code from Aweber – www.aweber.com

5. Install payment link (Visit www.FiveDayWeekend.com for an up-to-date listing of shopping cart software)

6. Install a toll-free number on my website for customer service calls

    a. Set up a free account with Freedom Voice – www.freedomvoice.com

Promotion and Follow Up System

1. Contact affiliates about new website
2. Write press release
    a. Hire freelancer from Guru.com – www.guru.com
3. Distribute press release
    a. PRWeb – www.prweb.com
4. Submit to search engines (Visit www.FiveDayWeekend.com for an up-to-date listing of search engine submission resources
5. Create a Facebook page and Twitter account
    a. Facebook – www.facebook.com
    b. Twitter – www.twitter.com
6. Write three follow-up sequence emails for Aweber

At our website www.FiveDayWeekend.com we have a complete 16 week coaching course that will provide additional training and weekly coaching to get you going even faster in your lifestyle business.

Income Leverage – Distribution – How to get an army of people to sell your products and services

Leveraging distribution is when you have other people selling your products and services. This group is vital to your success. They can provide incredible leverage to both your income and getting the word out about your products. The key to distribution leverage is you set it up once and your system will take of the rest. Of course, you need set everything up and provide oversight to ensure everything is running smoothly. So how do you ensure distribution success? The secret is to be positioned at the "bottleneck". What I mean by this is you need to be positioned at the "bottleneck" where customers are looking for products like yours.

For example, if you want start an affiliate program for your product your customers are not the end customers who are buying your product, but the affiliates who are promoting your products. In this example, the bottle neck is the affiliate platform providers.

Here is list of affiliate platforms you can use to get affiliates to sell your products or become an affiliate for another company. You can use these affiliate platforms for selling both digital and physical products. Since each affiliate platform offers unique niches and support, check them out and select the best ones for what you need.

- CJ – www.CJ.com Commission Junction
- Clickbank – www.clickbank.com
- Share a Sale - www.ShareASale.com
- LinkShare.com
- AdsMarket.com
- WebGains.com
- HydraNetwork.com
- ROIrocket.com
- MarketLeverage.com
- TradeDoubler.com
- MaxBounty.com
- MoreNiche.com
- PlatinumPartner.com
- IronOffers.com
- LinkConnector.com
- PantheraNetwork.com
- LogicalMedia.comAffiliateFuel.com
- PrimaryAds.com
- OfferWeb.com
- ClickXChange.com
- MarketHealth.com
- ClixGalore.com
- PepperJamNetwork.com
- CandadianSponsors.com
- AffiliateWindow.com
- Affiliatebot.com

Here are some of the bottleneck areas to help you get started to distribute your products:

- Affiliates platforms
  - See example list above
- Joint Venture Partners
  - Check out www.fivedayweekend.com for an up-to-date list of potential joint venture partners.
- Joint Venture Brokers
  - Check out www.fivedayweekend.com for an up-to-date list of joint venture brokers.
- Brokers – physical products sold to retail stores
  - Food Brokers - www.foodbrokers.org/associations-organizations/
  - National Association General Merchandise Representatives – www.nagmr.com Representing companies to the Drug, Mass Merchandise, and Food Trade.
- Wholesalers – physical products sold to retail stores and distributors
  - Check out www.fivedayweekend.com for an up-to-date list of offline distribution partners.
- Distributors – physical products sold to retail stores
  - Check out www.fivedayweekend.com for an up-to-date list of offline distribution partners.

Income Leverage – Fulfillment – How to get your product into your customers hands without you physically touching it

The next challenge we will outcome is how to get your product into your customers hand without you touching it. Here is a list of services you can use to fulfill digital and physical products.

Digital Product Fulfillment Strategies

Digital fulfillment services not only collect the money from your customers when they purchase your product but also provide the download link also. Your money is automatically deposited into your account.

- o Clickbank – www.clickbank.com
- o Lulu – www.lulu.com
- o CreateSpace – www.createspace.com

Physical Product Fulfillment Services

Fullfillment companies allow physical product ecommerce merchants to manage their businesses from anyplace on the globe. The handle packing, shipping product storage, order processing and more.

- o eFulfillment Service – www.efulfillmentservice.com
- o Shipwire – www.shipwire.com
- o AVC Corporation – www.avccorp.com
- o Webgistix – www.webgistix.com

CD/DVD, Print on Demand, Training Material Services

These companies will publish your CD/DVD and offer print on demand material. They can also ship your product directly to your customer for you.

- o Kunaki – www.kunaki.com
- o TrepStar.com - http://www.cd-fulfillment.com
- o Disk.com - www.disk.com
- o Speaker Fulfillment Services – www.speakerfilfullmentservices.com
- o Modern Fulfillment - www.modernfulfillment.com
- o Kindle Direct Publishing - http://forums.kindledirectpublishing.com/kdpforums/index.jspa

Dropshippers

Dropshipping is similar to being an affiliate. You are selling someone else's product on your website. You simply keep the spread between the retail cost and the wholesale cost. In addition to the wholesale cost, you would also pay a small dropship cost. The benefit to a dropship arrangement is you focus your time and effect selling the product and not packing and shipping the product.

- o Wordwide Brands www.worldwidebrands.com
- o Doba - www.doba.com

Bonus Material:

Getting the Cash Flow Mindset

When I chased after money, I never had enough. When I got my life on purpose and focused on giving of myself and everything that arrived into my life, then I was prosperous.

~ Wayne Dyer ~

Money should be used to fund your lifestyle; it should not be an end goal. If you spend your precious time chasing the goal of having a million dollars, you can easily forget why you are working so hard. I don't want you to fall into the trap many others have. I want you to enjoy a Five Day Weekends every week of the year.

As you learned previously, being a lifestyle entrepreneur is about using money to enjoy life on your terms. It's about funding your current lifestyle with an eye toward the future. It's about generating cash flow and not solely focusing on building net worth. You business is both generating the cash you need to live and building net worth in your future.

Consider most people look at life completely different. They are building net worth and not cash flow. They are putting money away in the stock market and buying real estate. As the previous decade has shown real estate doesn't always go up and the stock market does experience bear markets. That is the ebb and flow of asset investing. If you're in your mid-20's working in the corporate world with a goal of retiring in 40 years, the recent stock market volatile and crash of the housing market really doesn't affect you. However, if you're 5 years from retirement and the value of your portfolio is reduce to 30% and the value of your house (that you were planning on selling to fund your retirement) is sliced in half, you have a completely different point of view on what happened over the last 10 years.

If, for example, your goal is to have one million dollars in your bank account, before your start your lifestyle business you then have to ask yourself, "Will it be enough?" Let's look at the numbers. If you have one million dollars the day you get started, how much income will that produce? The goal is to have income produced by your assets to support your lifestyle. You can't afford to siphon off principal just to live.

Let's assume the million dollars will produce an annual return of 6 percent. In this example, your million dollars will produce $60,000 in annual cash flow.

$1,000,000 x 6% = $60,000
(Remember, you will not siphon off principal to support your lifestyle.)

Is that enough money to support your lifestyle? Only you can answer that question.

However, what happens to your dream if you don't achieve your million-dollar goal? The simple answer is, you won't do it. Your dream will end in quiet desperation. No matter how much you want to get started, if you have a net worth mentality, the million-dollar goal has tripped you up. Your calculations are based on having a million dollars prior to retiring, not in creating a lifestyle. That is why you need to create a cash flow requirement rather than a bank account size.

Cash flow is what determines your lifestyle, not net worth. I know many people who own several cars, three boats, and two houses. The asset side of their net worth indicates $750,000. However, when they factor in the liability side and calculate their true net worth, they have a negative $250,000. They simply own hundreds of thousands of dollars of "stuff."

What is "stuff?" Stuff is two boats, four snowmobiles, two sets of golf clubs and two BMW's. While owning them can be fun, you need to determine if your Five Day

Weekend requires them. Many people who own multiple piles of "stuff" must work just to keep a roof over their heads. They need to work 80 hours a week to pay for all the "stuff."

Many of them are so busy working they can't enjoy their "stuff" to the fullest. Although it appears they have everything, they lack the free cash flow to keep the wheels of their life rotating smoothly.

One of the greatest secrets that I learned from being in the financial services industry is that living in a big house doesn't make you rich. Many people falsely believe that someone who lives in a 5,000 square foot house overlooking the ocean or a golf course is rich. The truth is, some of these families have trouble making their monthly mortgage payments.

Many "cash flow-orientated" individuals and lifestyle entrepreneurs have no desire to live in a 5,000 square foot house and own seven cars. They have a different mindset. Cash flow-orientated people want to own a nice house, pay for the necessities of life and enjoy their free time. They chose how they want to produce a cash flow and enjoy life to the fullest. Instead of buying a new set of golf clubs for $2,000 they would rather spend that money on a two week "mini-retirement" in Mexico. They run their business from the rented condo, rent golf clubs and enjoy the best the area has to offer. They are in it for the experience and not for the most amount of toys they can own.

Design Your Ideal Lifestyle…Create A Lifestyle or a Job…It's Your Choice

Anyone can get a job and "earn a living." However, if you want to design a lifestyle, you need a plan. There is a big difference between earning a living and designing a lifestyle. Designing a lifestyle is not better than earning a living, nor is earning a living better than designing a lifestyle. They are just different. It is up to you to decide how you want to spend your time, talent and skills. However, my goal is to assist you in designing the lifestyle of your dreams.

A lifestyle allows you to enjoy life on your terms. It allows you to enjoy long walks on the beach, playing early-morning golf and spending countless hours skiing through the powder-white snow of the Utah slopes while you are running your business. A lifestyle gives you the free time to truly enjoy everything life has to offer.

Earning a living is exactly what it sounds like. You work to pay your bills. You work nights, weekends and any other shift to keep your family fed and gas in the car. Free time is a scarce resource. It doesn't matter how much money you make, anyone can be in the "earning a living" group. I know families that earn over $150,000 per year and still have a difficult time paying their bills. I once knew an individual who earned $50,000 in one month and declared bankruptcy the same month. The "earning a living" crowd always has "too much month left at the end of the money". They live from paycheck to paycheck. They have the best cars, live in the best neighborhoods and yet are cash poor.

To realize your Five Day Weekend to the fullest, you will want to convert your frame of mind. Begin to design a lifestyle instead of just earning a living.

Anyone can "earn a living," but if you want to truly enjoy the Five Day Weekend lifestyle, your financial affairs need to be in order.

You're lifestyle business will be generating cash flow and you need to manage that cashflow to fund your dream. Two vital steps in solidifying your future include learning how to create a cash flow statement and a household budget.

Get Your Financial House in Order

A cash flow statement is your first step. This financial statement shows you where your money is coming from (cash inflow) and where it is going (cash outflow). Once you have created a cash flow statement, you'll learn how create a household budget. Your budget will allocate your money to its highest and best use.

The best way to create a cash flow statement (CFS) is to record three months of your spending history, and compile this information in a cash flow statement. You will need to categorize your spending under specific headings. For example, under the heading of "personal care" on your cash flow statement, you could combine haircuts, shampoo, and cologne into one amount. This will allow you to simplify your statement. Also, once you've completed your CFS, you'll have a better idea of what you absolutely need on your life and what you may want to remove from your life.

For example, after you complete your CFS, you may realize your monthly credit cards payments consume 30% of your cash flow. If you want to enjoy "mini-retirements", maybe one of your financial goals would be to pay off your past so you can focus on your future.

Let's look at a sample cash flow statement for a hypothetical couple, John and Mary Smith. The Smiths' monthly cash flow statement begins on the following page.

Monthly Cash Flow Statement

For the Month of: September

Cash Inflow (Net)

Bonus

Dividends

Interest

Other income

Rental income

Net salary (Husband) $3,450.00

Net salary (Wife) $850.00

Total Monthly Income $4,300.00

Cash Outflow

General Expense

Auto maintenance/repair $86.00

Auto payments $764.00

Clothing $164.00

Credit card payments $170.00

Daycare $300.00

Entertainment $100.00

Gasoline $175.00

Tithe to church $60.00

Food Expense

 Dining out $440.00

 Groceries $340.00

 Miscellaneous (candy bars, etc.) $50.00

House Expense

  Maintenance $60.00

  Mortgage $760.00

  Rent payment

  Monthly tax amount $125.00

Insurance (monthly)

  Auto $150.00

  Health $194.00

  House $50.00

  Life $39.00

Utilities

  Electric $60.00

  Natural gas $75.00

  Telephone $65.00

  Water $45.00

Total Monthly Outflow $4,272.00

Total Surplus (Deficit) $28.00

As you can determine from the Smith's September cash flow statement, they have $28 remaining at the end of the month. I have included a blank cash flow statement for your use:

Monthly Cash Flow Statement

For the Month of: September

Cash Inflow (Net)

Bonus _____

Dividends _____

Interest _____

Other income _____

Rental income _____

Net salary (Husband) _____

Net salary (Wife) _____

Total Monthly Income _____

Cash Outflow

General Expense
Auto maintenance/repair _____

Auto payments _____

Clothing _____

Credit card payments _____

Daycare _____

Entertainment _____

Gasoline _____

Tithe to church _____

Food Expense
 Dining out _____

 Groceries _____

 Miscellaneous (candy bars, etc.) _____

House Expense
 Maintenance _____

 Mortgage/rent _____

 Monthly tax amount _____

Insurance (monthly)
 Auto _____

 Health _____

 House _____

Life   _____

Utilities

Electric   _____

Natural gas   _____

Telephone   _____

Water   _____

Total Monthly Outflow   _____

Total Surplus (Deficit)   _____

Now that you know the status of your cash flow, you need to create a monthly budget and get the remainder of your financial house in order. The previous example had the couple earning a salary, so is the amount couple would need to replace to start enjoying Five Day Weekends. This exercise shows exactly how much income is coming in and the expenses going out everything month. They need to decide what expenses are required for their new lifestyle and how much income is needed to support that lifestyle.

Create a Monthly Budget Allocation

A comprehensive budget will allow you to channel your financial resources toward your lifestyle. Without a budget, vast amounts of money may slip through your fingers and your dreams of being a lifestyle entrepreneur may not come true. Many people think they don't make enough money to create a budget. However, people who earn at least $25,000 per year will have over a million dollars pass through their hands over a 40 year career. This is a tremendous amount of money.

The chart below demonstrates how much money an individual may earn over an average working lifetime. I call this amount that you will be redirecting *Lifestyle Cash*.

This is the amount of cash you have to fund your lifestyle. This exercise gives you a definite goal for the amount of money that will be available to you over your lifetime.

Years Working	Yearly Income	*Lifetime Cash*
40	$25,000	$1,000,000
30	$50,000	$1,500,000
20	$85,000	$1,700,000

As you can see, an individual making $25,000 per year will earn $1,000,000 over a 40-year career. That is a substantial amount of money passing this individual's way. To approximate your *Lifetime Cash*, use the formula below:

Years Working x Yearly Income   =   *Lifetime Cash*

_____   X   _____   =   _____

Many people who initially use the above formula are astonished with the amount of money they might earn over their working lifetime. After you determine how much money will be coming your way, doesn't it make sense to try to keep, enjoy and invest as much of it as possible?

Monthly Transaction Record Sheets

To keep track of your cash flow, record your expenses on a Monthly Transaction Record Sheet. Think of this sheet as a financial diary. First you write down a description of any purchases and the amount spent, then indicate if you paid cash, wrote a check or used a credit card. By recording how you paid for the transaction and what you bought, you will track how and where you spend money.

To get a good sampling, use this method for at least three months. Even better is a year's worth of records. This method is designed to give you an accurate and true picture of your spending habits. It also provides an overview of how you are spending your money. Are you using cash, credit cards, debit cards or writing checks? You'll soon find that enjoying Five Day Weekends, you'll probably be using your credit cards and debit cards for the majority of your purchases. The reason is you don't want to carry large amounts of cash with you and purchases made on credit or debit cards can also be disputed if you receive a product or service that is not satisfactory. In addition, you'll want to start paying off your credit cards. They reason is many credit cards charge an annual interest rate of 20% or more. The money that you would pay for interest expense to the credit card company will now be used to fund your lifestyle. I'll provide a proven method to help you pay off your credits in the quickest time possible. I first published this strategy in 1999 and it is called "The Debt Reduction Pyramid".

To replace your credit cards, you'll want to open a debit card account and I recommend you get a PayPal MasterCard debit card. This is a debit card that is directly linked to your PayPal account. Since your business will accept PayPal payments, you know you'll always being have cash deposited into your Paypal account. You can use your PayPal debit card worldwide at ATM's, online or anywhere MasterCard is accepted.

Here is a brief overview of the benefits of the PayPal MasterCard debit card directly from the PayPal website:

"The PayPal Debit Card is the fastest way to get money out of your PayPal account.

- Use it worldwide at ATMs, online, or anywhere MasterCard is accepted
- Earn 1% cash back whenever you sign for a purchase[1]
- Enjoy 100% protection against unauthorized charges to your card"

www.PayPal.com

Here is a sample Monthly Transaction Record for John and Mary Smith. The Smiths want to start their Lifestyle Business immediately.

The first step they took was to begin recording their purchases on a Monthly Transaction Record Sheet. Both John and Mary used a Transaction Record Sheet for three months. Once the three-month period was over, they combined their results into one sheet. The following is a sampling from the combined Transaction Record Sheet for the Smiths:

Monthly Transaction Record Sheet

For the Month of: July

Date	Description of Transaction	Amount Paid	Cash	Check	Credit Card	Debit Card
7/1	Groceries	$25.00	X			
7/1	Gasoline for car	$12.00			X	
7/1	Kid's clothes	$74.00		X		
7/2	Candy bar	$.95	X			
7/2	New pair of shoes	$57.00				X
7/6	Lunch at deli	$13.48			X	
7/6	Dinner out	$29.77			X	
7/6	New blouse	$85.64			X	
7/10	New couch	$780.00			X	
7/15	Car repairs - Brakes	$412.00			X	
7/15	Paid credit card bill	$170.00		X		
7/15	Paid day care bill	$325.00			X	
7/15	Diapers	$89.54				X
7/15	Tithe to church	$30.00	X			
7/20	Dinner out	$79.71			X	
7/25	New cordless drill	$250.00		X		

The sample of the Smith's expenses demonstrates how quickly a family's income can seem to evaporate. Note the $13.48 spent on a deli lunch. If you are going to keep an accurate record of your expenses, no expense should be overlooked regardless of size.

Monthly Transaction Record Sheets work. The first time my wife Jennifer and I completed and reviewed our Monthly Transaction Record Sheets, we were amazed at how much money slipped through our fingers. For example, we bought snacks and soft drinks and ate lunch at one of the local restaurants on a daily basis. Without realizing it, we were spending 15 percent of our monthly take-home income on frivolous items. By using a Monthly Transaction Record Sheet, we were able to see how we were spending our money and began to take control of our finances. Monthly Transaction Record Sheet

For the Month of: _____

Date Description of Transaction	Amount Paid	Cash	Check	Credit Card	Debit Card

Note: Visit our website www.FiveDayWeekend.com to learn how to obtain a blank cash flow statement.

Another great way to keep track of your daily transactions is to use a spreadsheet program on a computer. Type in all the headings for your transactions at the top of the spreadsheet, and just input your spending information at the end of each day. The computer program will keep track of all your purchases and automatically enable you to add them up quickly at the end of three months.

Once you have completed Monthly Transaction Sheets for a period of three months, you will have enough information about your spending habits to develop a monthly budget. The purpose of a budget is to redirect any portion of your income that is currently slipping through your fingers into your bank account.

Create an Emergency Fund

If you don't already have it, the first line item you need to add to your household budget is "Emergency Fund." An emergency fund is another vital element to building your Lifestyle Business. Many financial planners say a family should stash away at least six months of expenses into an emergency fund. However, three to four months of expenses is more realistic. Your emergency fund provides that extra piece of mind. If you're across the country or across the globe and an emergency occurs, you'll have this account to us.

The account should be funded on a monthly basis, just like any other expense. Once you have three or more months of expenses in this account, you will stop funding it.

Should you run into an emergency prior to funding your emergency account, here are six suggestions for how to obtain money in a relatively short amount of time:

1. Overdraft Protection
Place overdraft protection on your checking account. Overdraft protection prevents a check from being returned for non-sufficient funds. Overdraft protection is a loan made by the bank to you should you accidentally write a check greater than the funds in your checking account. The overdraft loan from the bank is usually paid back in

monthly installments. Depending on your credit score and relationship with your bank, most financial institutions allow overdraft protection from $250 - $5,000.

2. Establish a Line of Credit

An open line of credit, also known as a signature loan, is an unsecured loan that has already been approved by the bank. To open a line of credit, you need to visit your local bank and complete the necessary paperwork.

3. Use Secured Loans

A secured loan is a loan secured by another asset. For example, if you have a $1,000.00 certificate of deposit (CD), you could obtain a loan for approximately $1,000.00 by using your CD as collateral.

4. Tap Your Home Equity

If you are a homeowner consider obtaining a home equity loan that offers check-writing privileges. It's a great way to have funds available for an emergency. A home equity loan amount is usually 75 to 80 percent of the value of your home, less what you currently owe on the home. However, in the recent real estate market decline, this may be harder to achieve.

You need to fill out all of the home equity paperwork with the bank or mortgage company. Once everything is complete, the bank can give you a checkbook instead of a lump sum for your monetary needs. By having check writing privileges, you can write checks for any amount up to the pre-determined limit. The interest for this type of loan may also be tax deductible. Check with your tax advisor.

5. Credit Card Cash Advances

Use this option only as a last resort. The unfavorable interest rates on most cash advances make this option cost prohibitive.

6. Sell Your Receivables

This is called factoring. Factoring is when a business sells it account receivables at a discount. This is an excellent way to get a large amount of cash in a short amount of time. Use this option as the last resort, but you have it available if you need it.

Monitor Your Progress

Once you have organized your finances into an easy-to-follow format, you will need to monitor your progress continually. One of the best ways is to use an annual net worth statement. Your net worth is what you own reduced by what you owe. The formula for net worth is:

Total Assets - Total Liabilities = Net Worth

For example, if you have $50,000.00 in assets and $45,000.00 in liabilities your net worth is $5,000.00. Assets are cash, real estate, personal property, etc. A liability is any outstanding debt. Since most people would not liquidate 100% of their assets to pay off their liabilities, calculating your net worth is a "textbook" type of exercise, but it serves to provide an indication of the direction of your financial progress. The best time to do your net worth statement is in December or January. During this time of year most people are creating goals for the coming year. In fact, a great New Year's resolution is to increase your net worth by 10 percent each year. I have included a blank net worth statement on the following pages for your use.

Net Worth Statement

Date: /   /

Assets

Liquid Assets (Short-term Assets)

Checking account: $_____

Cash value of life insurance policy _____

Money market account: _____

Savings account: _____

Household Assets (Long-term Assets)

Antiques: $_____

Automobile #1:   _____

Automobile #2: _____

Clothes: _____

Dishes: _____

Furniture: _____

Home computer system: _____

Home entertainment center: _____

House: _____

Jewelry: _____

Other real estate holdings: _____

Recreational vehicles: (boats, jet skis, snowmobiles, etc.) _____

Tools: _____

Investment and Retirement Assets (Long-term Assets)
Bonds: $_____

Company retirement plan #1: _____

Company retirement plan #2: _____

Individual retirement account #1: _____

Individual retirement account #2: _____

Mutual funds: _____

Stocks: _____

Other: _____

Total Assets (Short-term Assets + Long-term Assets)

$_____$

Liabilities

Short-term Liabilities (Paid off in 3 years or less)

Automobile loan #1: $_____

Automobile loan #2:   _____

Credit card payments: _____

Medical bills: _____

Student loans: _____

Long-term Liabilities

Home mortgage: $_____

Notes payable: _____

Other real estate loans: _____

Total Liabilities (Short-term Liabilities + Long-term Liabilities)

$_____

Net Worth (Total Assets − Total Liabilities)

$_____

Note: Visit our website www.FiveDayWeekend.com to learn how to obtain a blank Net Worth Statement.

In addition to an annual net worth statement, you should also create an annual Cash Flow Statement (simply a summary of your monthly cash flow statements). This annual Cash Flow Statement allows you to make any necessary changes to your budget. For example, at the end of December you may realize that you are not budgeting enough throughout the year for your holiday expenses.

Eliminate Your Financial Past

Can I pay my Visa payment with my MasterCard?

~ Author Unknown ~

Credit card debt is a national dilemma and the most cunning adversary to securing your dreams of enjoying the Five Day Weekend lifestyle. Many credit card companies use enticing promotions to lure consumers into using credit cards by increasing credit limits and offering pre-approved credit cards with great introductory rates. All of these offers are an attempt to install the habit of spending now and paying later.

Unfortunately, most people don't realize how destructive this habit is until their credit card payments become the largest part of their monthly budget. Credit card debt, as a percentage of income, has been on the rise for the past two decades. No matter how difficult it may be to break the habit of credit card debt, the reward is worth the effort.

One debt reducing strategy is what I call "The Debt Elimination Pyramid." By using this debt elimination strategy, you will be able to completely pay off your credit card balances and get started on the road to securing your financial future.

The Debt Elimination Pyramid

The Debt Elimination Pyramid is designed to help you pay off your credit card balances as quickly and painlessly as possible. For example, if you wanted to tear down a pyramid, where would you start? The most logical place to start is at the tip of the pyramid, since the foundation is so tremendous. You would begin at the top of the pyramid and remove one brick at a time until the entire pyramid had been torn down. That is the same method you will follow to remove all of your credit card balances. Credit card debt is destroyed one payment at a time. There are four simple steps in the Debt Elimination Pyramid.

1. Write down all of your credit card outstanding balances in ascending order (smallest to largest). For example, if you have four different credit cards, all with outstanding balances, you will write down the lowest to the highest balance on a sheet of paper. This is referred to as your Debt Pyramid.

2. Concentrate on completely paying off the card with the lowest balance. By paying off your lowest credit card balance, you eliminate the tip of your debt pyramid. You will pay as much as you can financially afford over and above the minimum payment required. For example, if the minimum monthly payment is $40 on your smallest balance, you could write a check for $75 ($40 minimum required plus an additional $35). You pay this extra amount every month until the entire balance of the first card is paid off.

3. Once the first credit card is completely paid off, concentrate on the next tier. After you have completely paid off the credit card balance at the tip of your pyramid, you will add the minimum monthly payment of your first card to the minimum monthly payment of your second smallest credit card. For example, if the minimum payment for your first position credit card was $40 and the payment for the second position card is $55, then your monthly payment to the second credit card will be $95 ($40 +$55 = $95). Just as you did with the first credit card, you are now eliminating the balance of the second card at a faster pace than you would if you just paid the minimum monthly amount required. In addition, the original total minimum payment requirement was already allocated into your budget. Thus, you will not need to allocate any additional money to pay off your total debt. This step of the strategy will decrease the time required to reduce your overall credit card balance.

4. Repeat steps one through three until all of your credit cards are completely paid off.

For example, Kim and Don Sanders, are using the Debt Elimination Pyramid Strategy to pay off their credit card debt. They have seven credit cards with total monthly combined payments of $855. Their outstanding balance is $27,500. They want to eliminate their credit card debt completely.

The first step Kim and Don took was to write down the outstanding balances of each credit card in ascending order. They also included the minimum monthly payment requirement for each credit card.

Here is what Don and Kim Sanders' Debt Pyramid looks like:

Debt Elimination Pyramid Worksheet

Credit Card Name	Outstanding Balance	Minimum Payment
Credit card #1	$1,575.00	$85.00
Credit card #2	$1,900.00	$110.00
Credit card #3	$2,374.00	$165.00
Credit card #4	$2,596.00	$130.00
Credit card #5	$3,750.00	$240.00
Credit card #6	$10,551.00	$295.00

Use the Debt Elimination Pyramid worksheet on the following page to write down your current outstanding credit card balances in ascending order.

Debt Elimination Pyramid Worksheet

Credit Card Name Outstanding Balance Minimum Payment

_____ $_____ $_____

_____ $_____ $_____

_____ $_____ $_____

_____ $_____ $_____

_____ $_____ $_____

_____ $_____ $_____

_____ $_____ $_____

_____ $_____ $_____

Note: Visit our website www.FiveDayWeekend.com to learn how to obtain a blank Debt Elimination Pyramid worksheet.

Now that you have created your own pyramid, follow the four steps in the Debt Elimination Pyramid Strategy to eliminate your credit card debt completely.

Another popular debt elimination approach many people follow is to pay off the credit card charging the highest rate of interest first. Once this card is paid off, they pay off the next highest interest rate. On the surface, this may seem like the best approach. However, when reviewing all the factors involved, it may be the toughest to follow.

While it is true that, by using either method, you are decreasing the total amount of time you are carrying balances on your credit card by making monthly payments over and above the minimum requirement, the length of time required to pay off a large balance can be frustrating to many people. By using my method, you receive an enormous psychological benefit each time one of your cards gets paid off. You will feel that you have torn off the top of the pyramid and can see the light at the end of your tunnel of debt. This alone can be enough encouragement to last you throughout the process of breaking the chains of debt.

How to Stop Using Your Credit Cards

Once you begin conquering your credit card balances, the worst thing to do is to begin using the cards again. Here are four approaches to help you stop using your credit cards:

1. Lock Up or Cut Up Your Credit Cards

The best way to stop using your credit cards is not to carry them. Once your debts are paid, eliminate all but one of your credit cards. The card you keep is for emergency use only, since there may be times when you will need to have access to a large amount of purchasing power on short notice. For example, you may need to replace the engine in your car or buy an airplane ticket in a family emergency. An innovative way to remember that your credit card is for emergency use only is to tape a piece of paper to your credit card with the words: "FOR EMERGENCY USE ONLY."

2. Write Checks

Get in the habit of writing checks for all of your purchases. This offers two advantages. The first benefit is that you can't make a purchase unless you have the money in your checking account. This may eliminate frivolous spending. The second advantage is that you will get out of the habit of using your credit cards.

3. Use Debit Cards

If you don't like writing checks, get a debit card. A debit card is similar to a credit card with one distinct difference. Whenever you make a purchase with a debit card, the money is immediately subtracted from your checking account. You cannot spend more than you have in your bank account. Make sure to write down your spending in your check register!

4. Reward Yourself When You Pay Off a Credit Card

Every time you pay off an outstanding balance, treat yourself to a long walk on the beach or a dinner out.

Five Day Weekend Coaching

If you're interested in learning how to leverage your time and your income to achieve the ultimate lifestyle, I do have limited space available in my personal one-on-one personal coaching?

Call my toll-free number at 1-877-746-7477 and ask for Jen to schedule an appointment.

www.ingramcontent.com/pod-product-compliance
Lightning Source LLC
Chambersburg PA
CBHW081726220526
45468CB00008B/1988